HOW TO DRAW
the
NeoPopRealism
ABSTRACT

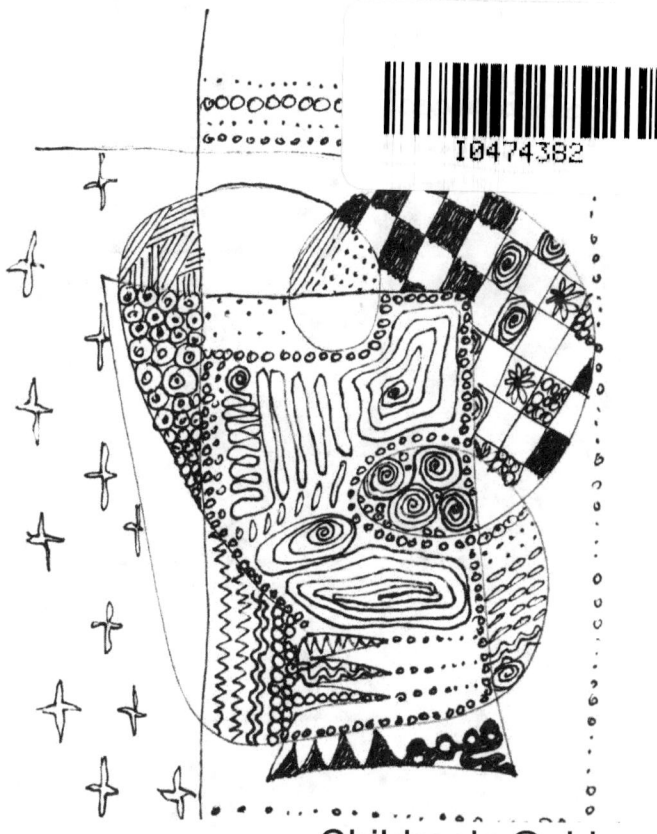

Children's Guide
NADIA RUSS
NeoPopRealism PRESS

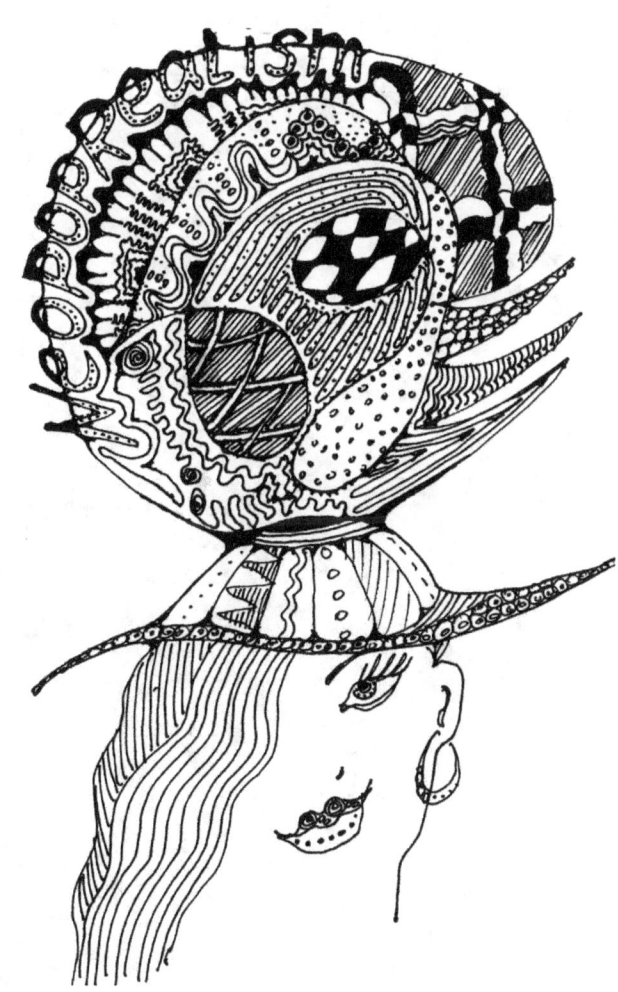

This girl is your hostess, she is Nadia Russ' assistant, and she will guide you through pages of this book. Her name is Neo (aka New).

HOW TO DRAW
the
NeoPopRealism
ABSTRACT

Children's Guide

NADIA RUSS
NeoPopRealism PRESS

First time published in 2011 by NeoPopRealism PRESS
PO BOX 366
New York, NY, 10013

NeoPopRealismPRESS@mail.com

 How to Draw the NeoPopRealism Abstract: Children's Guide by Nadia Russ

Illustrated by Nadia Russ

ISBN-13: 978-0615545332
ISBN-10: 0615545335

11 12 13 14 15 10 9 8 7 6 5 4 3 2 1

Published in the United States of America
Language English

This book teaches children how to draw whimsical NeoPopRealism abstract images using ink pen.

www.neopoprealism.org

CONTENT

INTRODUCTION

NeoPopRealism ink drawing style (learn how to pronounce it correctly: Neo-Pop-Realism) was created by Nadia Russ in 1989.

Nadia loves to experiment. Why? Because experiment is always adventure! You should love to experiment too. With this book, you will find out how to draw with ink pen images "Sky at Night", "Hurricane and Sun", and "Zig and Zag". You will learn how to draw without eraser.

You will use the same, but simplified, method of the drawing as *Nadia Russ* used first time 22 years ago, when she created this art style. Then, *Nadia Russ* imagined that her consciousness left her body and flew to the Space. Why she did it? She loved an idea of being united with the Universe. *Nadia Russ* thought it will help her create something new, like no human being created before.

Then, when her consciousness was in Space, her body was in her apartment in Moscow. While her consciousness was in Space, Nadia Russ' hand created the line, which was flowing freely. Then, appeared sections her hand filled with the repetitive patterns - circles, triangles, squares, rectangles, dots, zigzags and their different combinations and variations.

At that moment, *Universe* used *Nadia Russ* as a *Conductor* to create some absolutely amazing artwork.

Nadia didn't use eraser, because if a 'mistake' made, the following patterns balance the whole composition. Her drawing was unique; no artist did anything like this before. Later, she also began painting with acrylic on canvas, using the same concept.

January 4, 2003, in the United States, *Nadia Russ* created a word *NeoPopRealism* and internationally announced new style of visual arts.

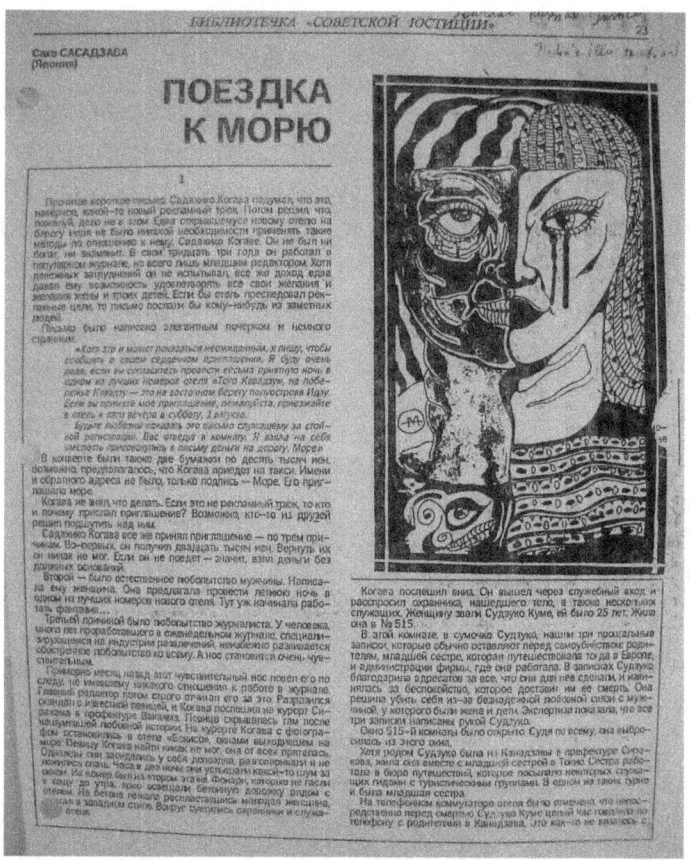

This is one of Nadia Russ' first ink drawings. It was published in *"Russian Justice"* Journal in Moscow, in 1992

TOOLS

Now, when you know what NeoPopRealism art is, learn about the tools. It won't be complicated. All you need is the black ink pen *Foray Rolle Rollerball Medium 0.7 mm, Sharpie* or any similar. It can be thinner or thicker pen, all depend on what you would like to draw. Also you need a piece of cardstock paper 8.5"x11" or any other size or type of paper. Again, all depend on what you would like to achieve and what is purpose for your drawing. Pen and paper can be purchased in Office Depot stores or in any convenience store locally.

We offer you to start drawing here, on special blank pages of this book. Simply follow the instructions. Also, you can try to finish each incomplete drawing you will find in this book.

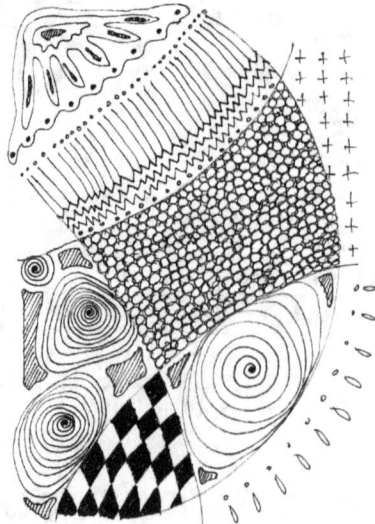

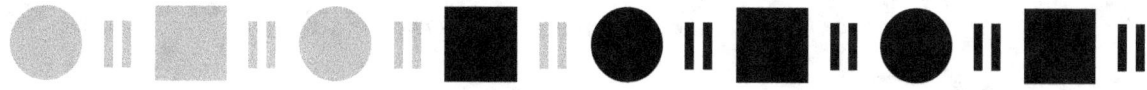

How to draw NeoPopRealism abstract "Hurricane & Sun"

Let's start your exiting journey to the world of NeoPopRealism with drawing an abstract "Hurricane & Sun."

What do you know about Hurricane and Sun? A hurricane is intense, rotating oceanic weather system. It possesses maximum sustained winds exceeding 74 mph; it forms over tropical oceanic regions. Hurricanes are smaller than storms; they are typically about 311 miles in diameter. At the ocean surface, the air spirals inward in a counterclockwise direction. This circulation becomes weaker with height, turning into clockwise outflow. The hurricanes are given names.

Sun is the star, it looks like a big ball of burning fire. Sun is located at the center of Solar System. It almost perfectly spherical and consists of magnetic fields and hot plasma. It has diameter of 1,392,000 kilometers, about 109 times that of Earth. The Sun is the brightest object in the sky. The distance between Sun and Earth is 149.6 million kilometers.

The following pages will show you step-by-step how to draw with ink pen image "Hurricane and Sun", which includes the abstract elements. Every following picture contains new details. Remember: no eraser needed. When you draw abstract images, you express your feelings, emotions and thoughts without drawing a realistic image. First draw lines, then fill sections with repetitive patterns. Always determine the mood of drawing.

The complete image looks like this:

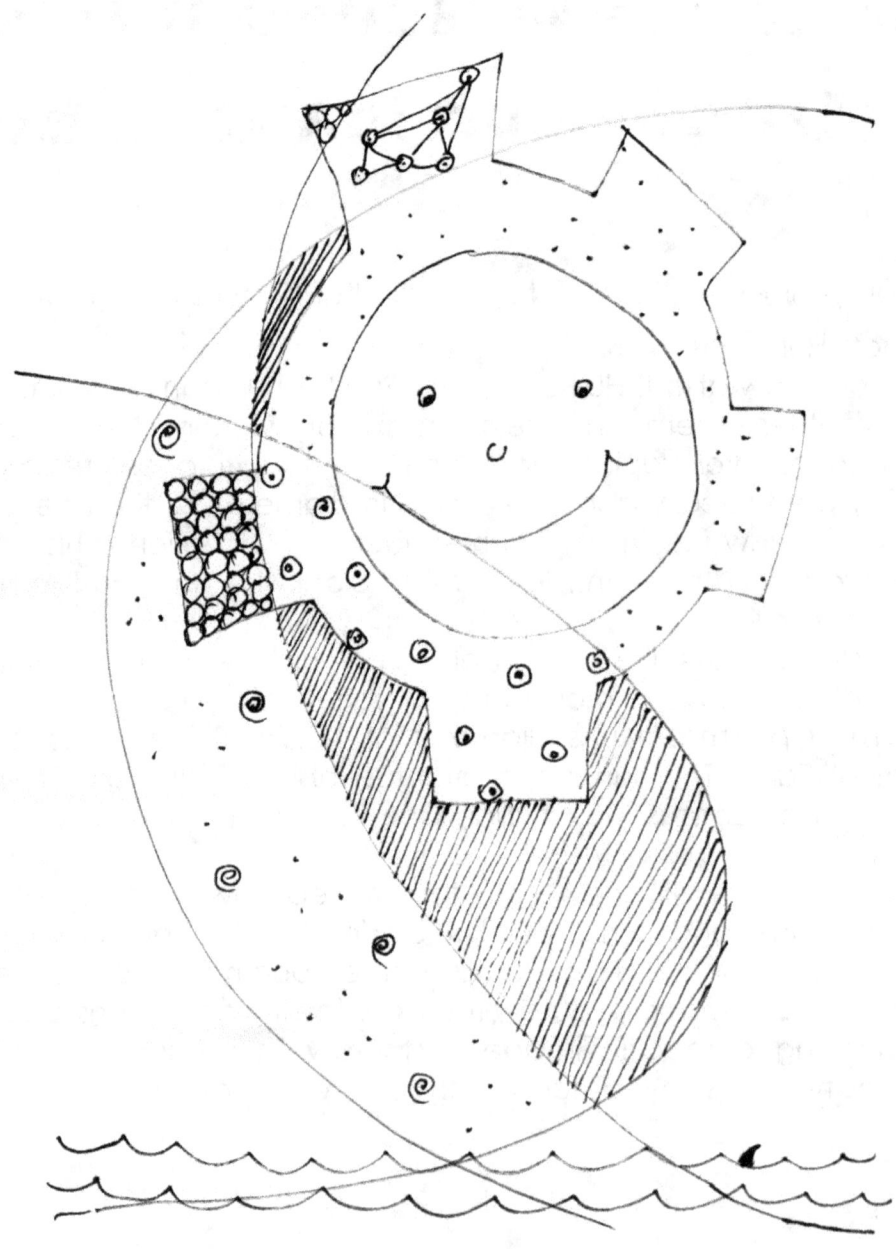

Hurricane & Sun, Ink on paper

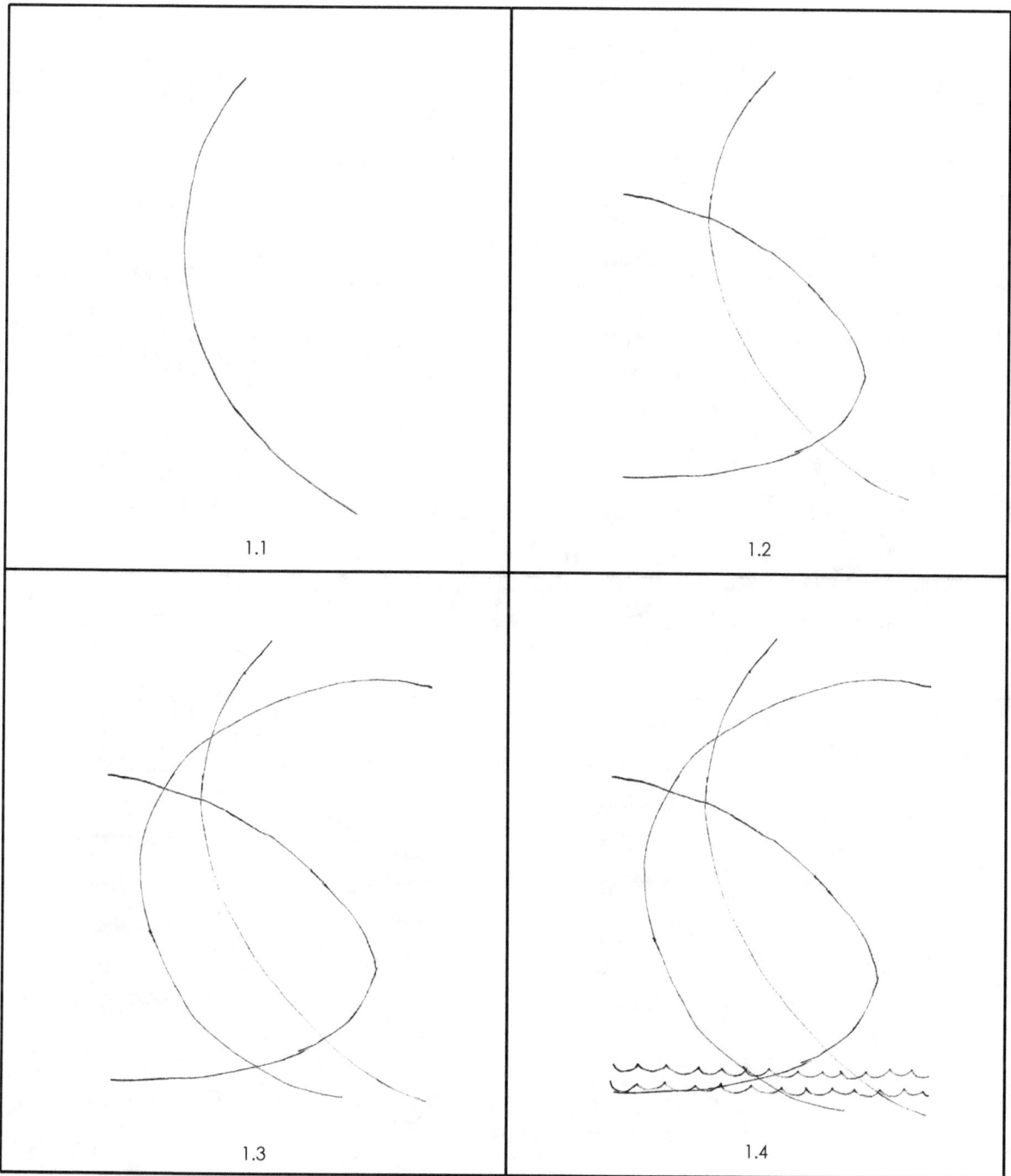

1.1

1.2

1.3

1.4

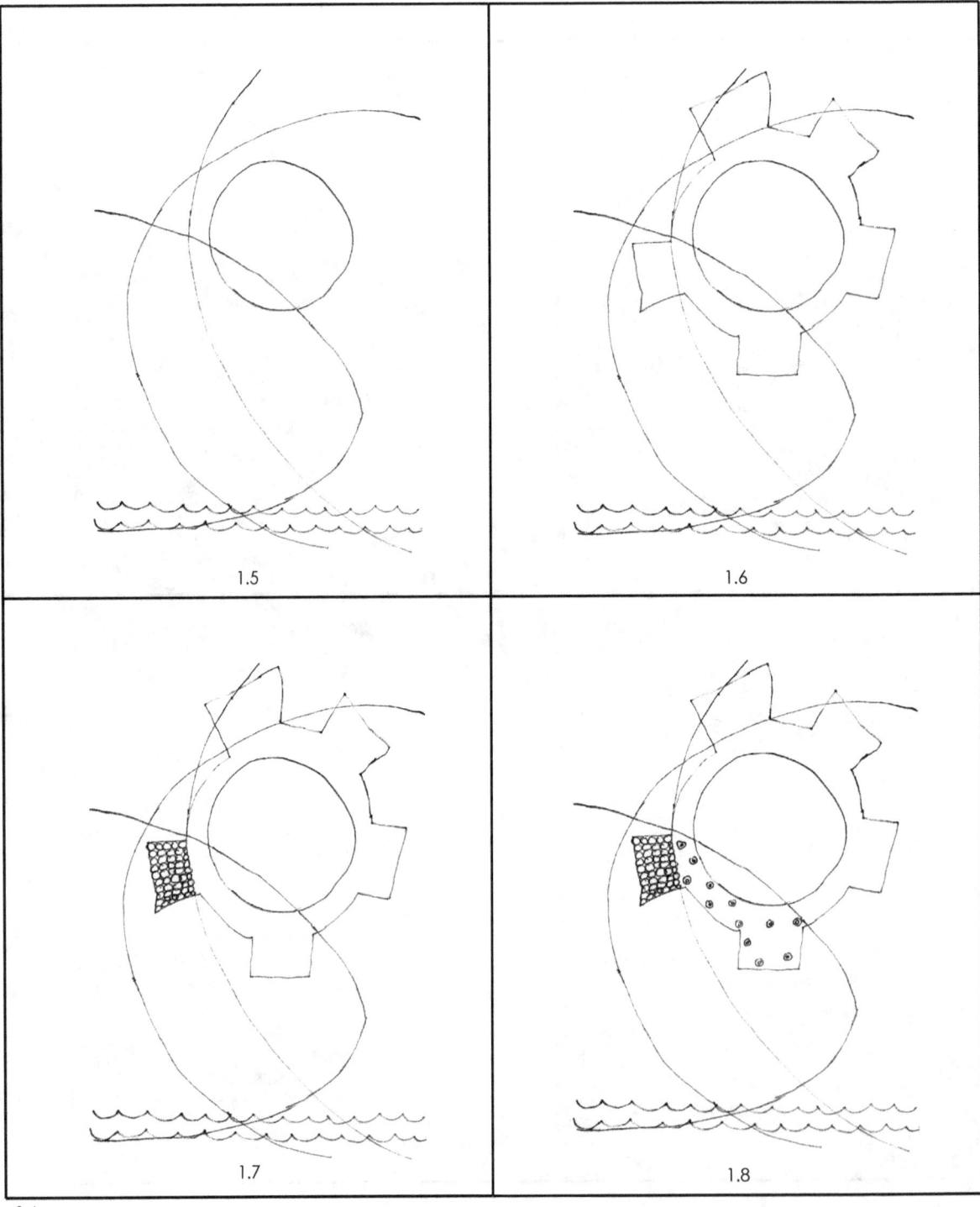

1.5

1.6

1.7

1.8

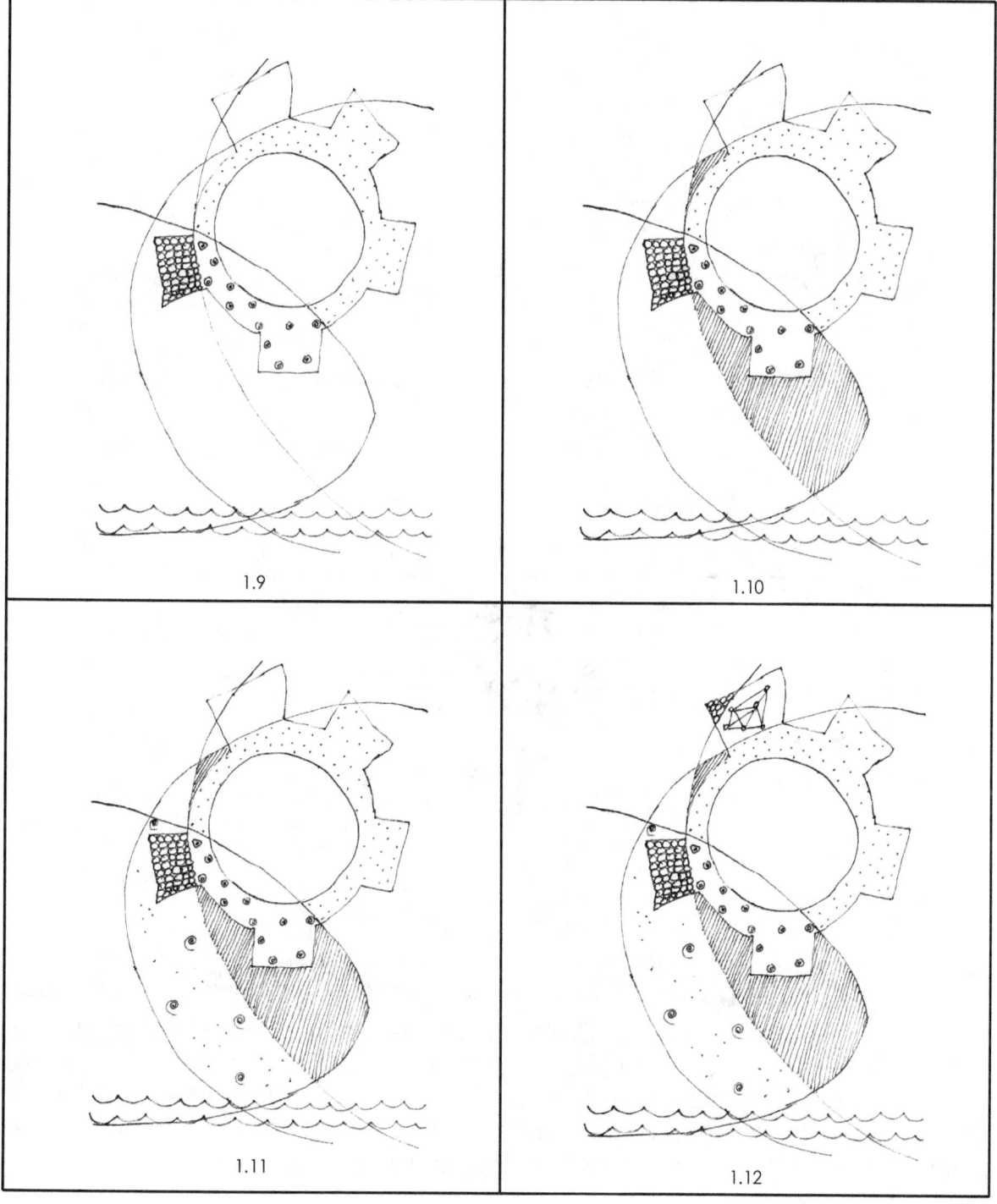

1.9

1.10

1.11

1.12

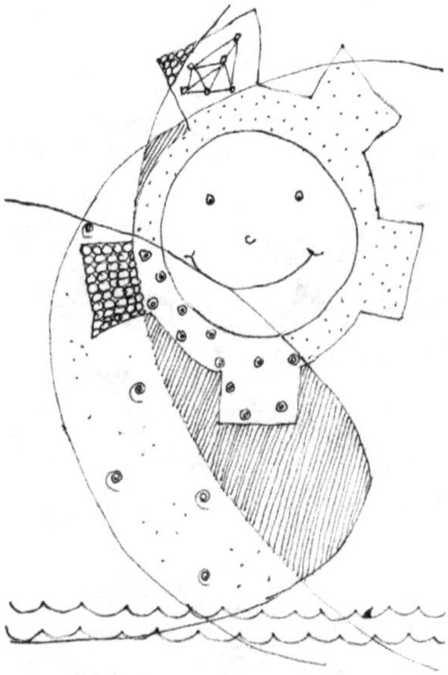

1.13

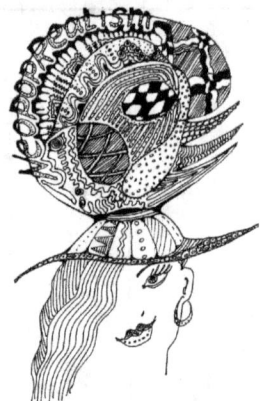

Neo: The following pages show you how to draw repetitive patterns, used in drawing "Hurricane & Sun." You can create the patterns using your imagination. The patterns can include the dots, circles ☐, squares ☐, triangles ☐, zigzags, and their combinations in any variations. But now, you will learn the very simple patterns. Later, after you learn how to draw the simple patterns, you will be able to create those, more complicated.

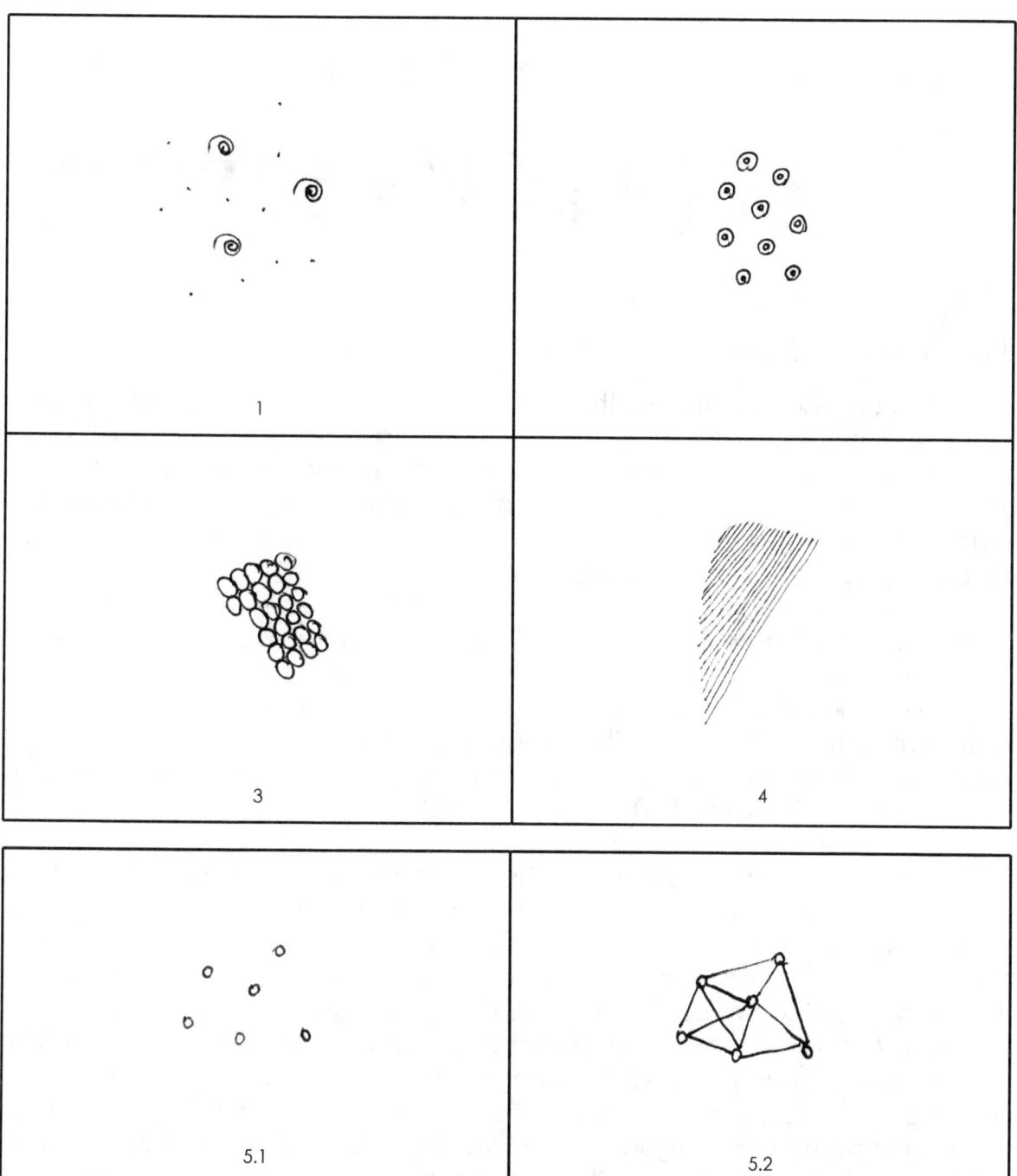

How to Draw image
"Sky at Night"

Did you ever saw the sky at night? I am sure you did. You saw Moon and a lot of stars. Moon is the Earth's natural satellite, it is the second brightest object in the sky after the Sun. The Moon orbits around the Earth. In 1959, first time people reached the Moon. It was the Soviet Union's spacecraft Luna 2. It was the year, when Nadia Russ was born. The most of the rocks on the surface of the Moon are between 4.6 and 3 billion years old. The Moon has no atmosphere and no global magnetic fields.

The stars are the massive balls of plasma held together by gravity. They vary in size, mass and temperature. Stars' diameters vary from 450x smaller to over 1000x larger than that of the Sun. The surface temperature can range from 3,000 to 50,000 Celsius. Different stars have different brightness. There are 6,000 stars potentially visible with unaided eye, but not at the same time. The total number of stars in the known universe is 70 sextillion - 70,000 million million million - 70,000 000 000 000 000 000 000.

The following pages will show you how with ink pen step-by-step to draw image "Sky at Night." Every following picture includes new details. Remember that you use no eraser. If a 'mistake' made, it will 'disappear' with the following repetitive patterns which will make your drawing beautiful and its composition balanced. The drawing "Sky at Night" contains elements of abstract. Abstract is artwork, filled with your emotions, thoughts, and feelings, but without drawing a realistic image. Always determine the mood of drawing. First, you will draw the lines. These lines carry the elements of abstract drawing and organize your drawing into sections, which later you will fill with repetitive patterns. The complete image will look like one on the right.

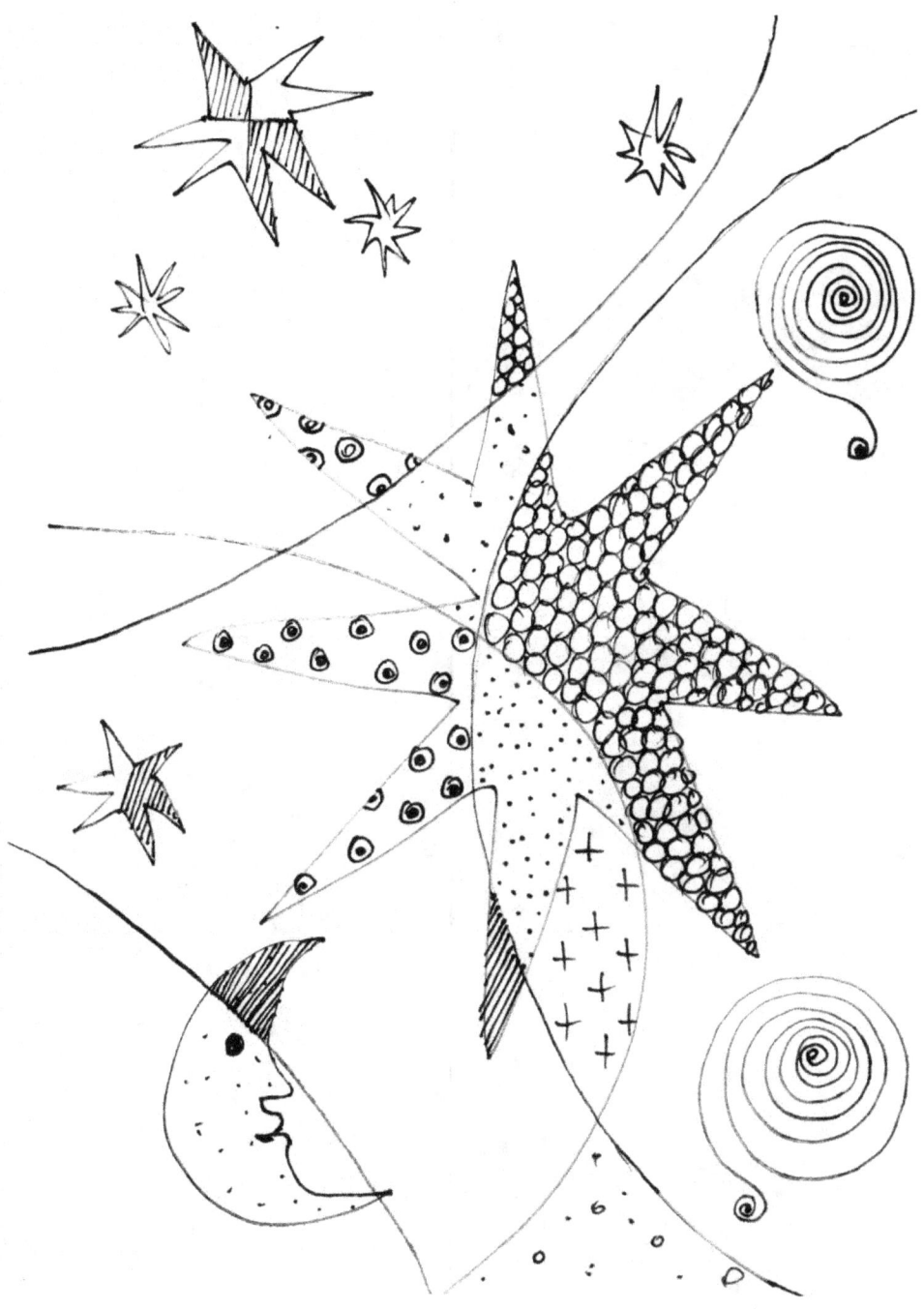

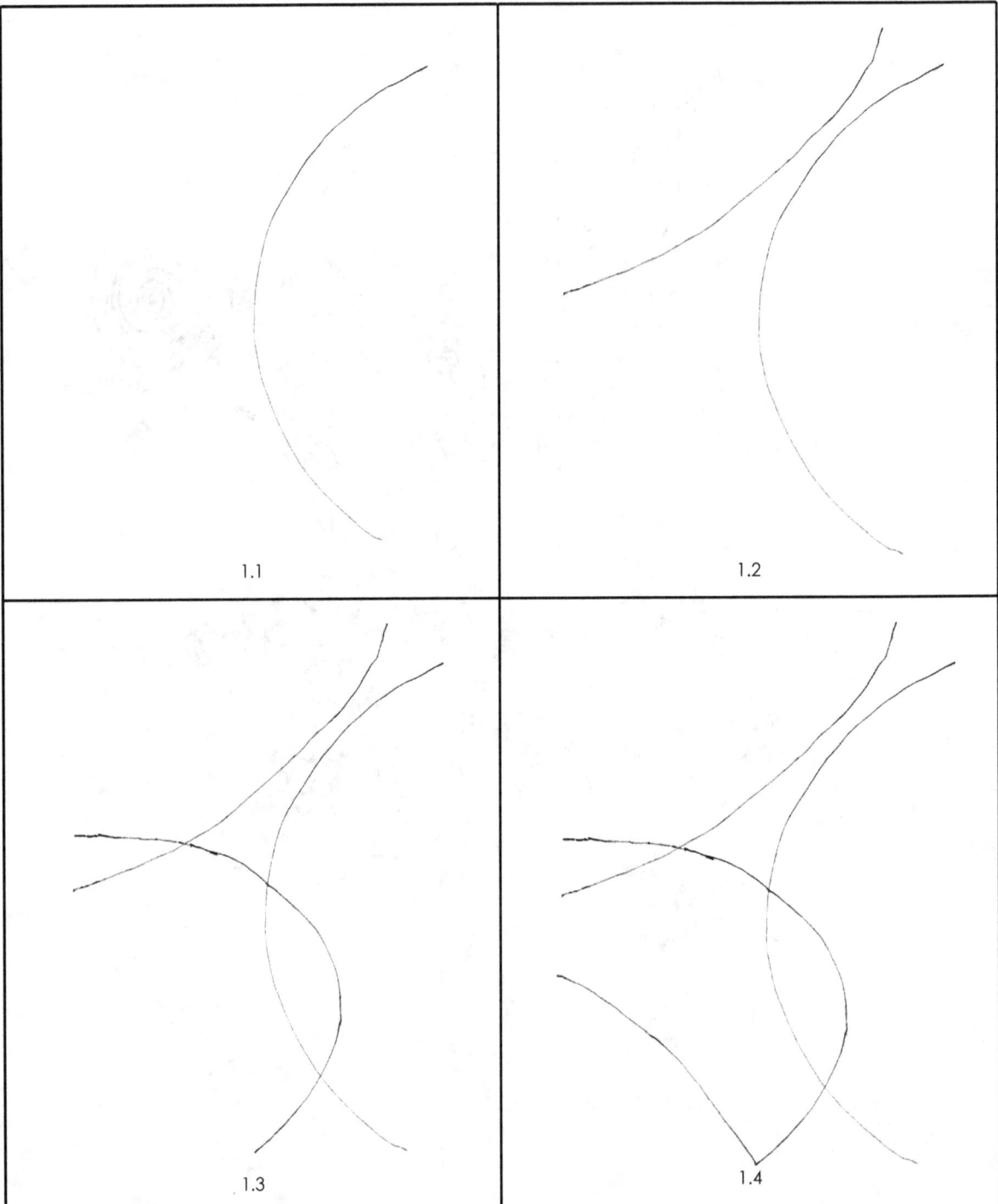

1.1

1.2

1.3

1.4

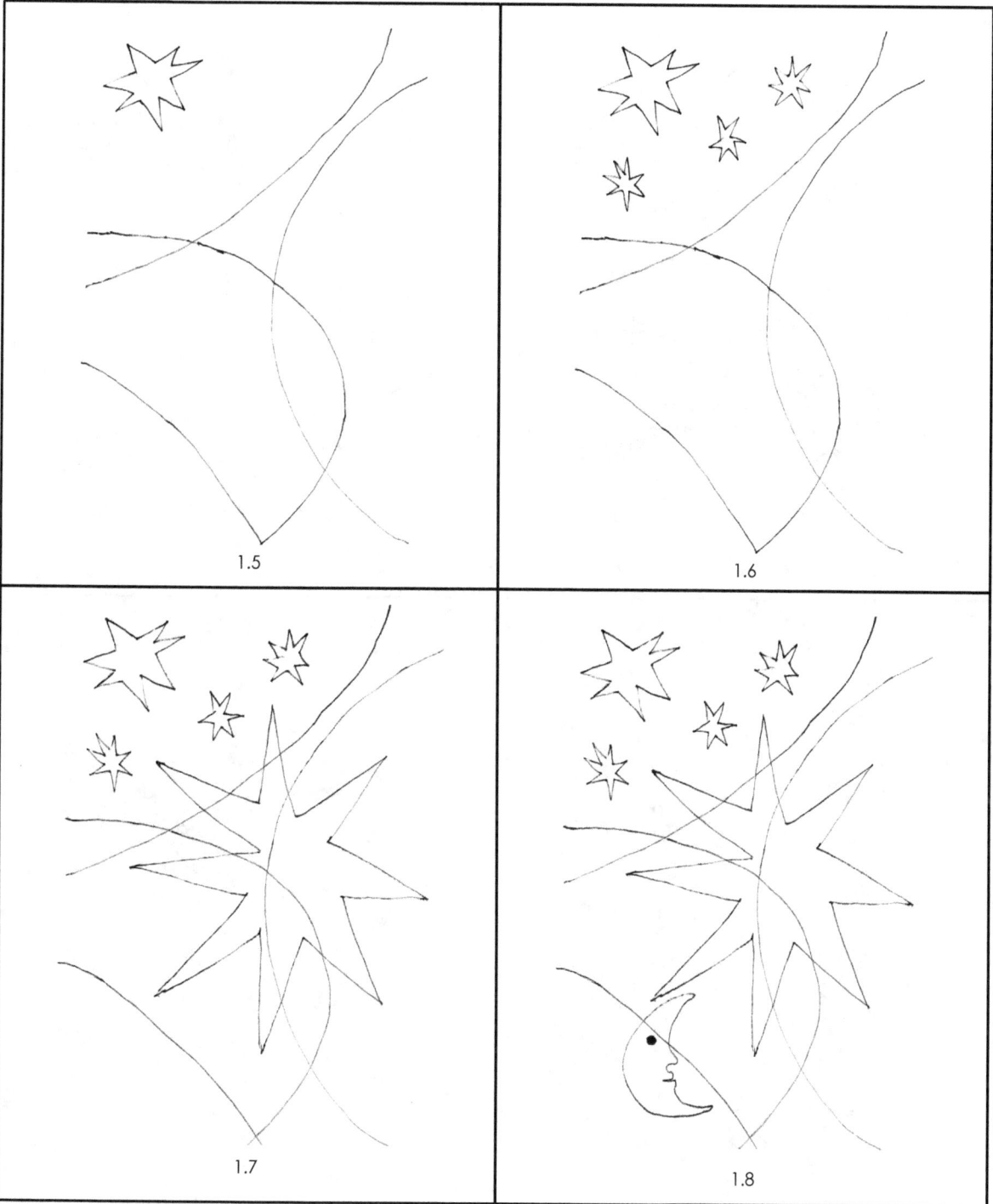

1.5

1.6

1.7

1.8

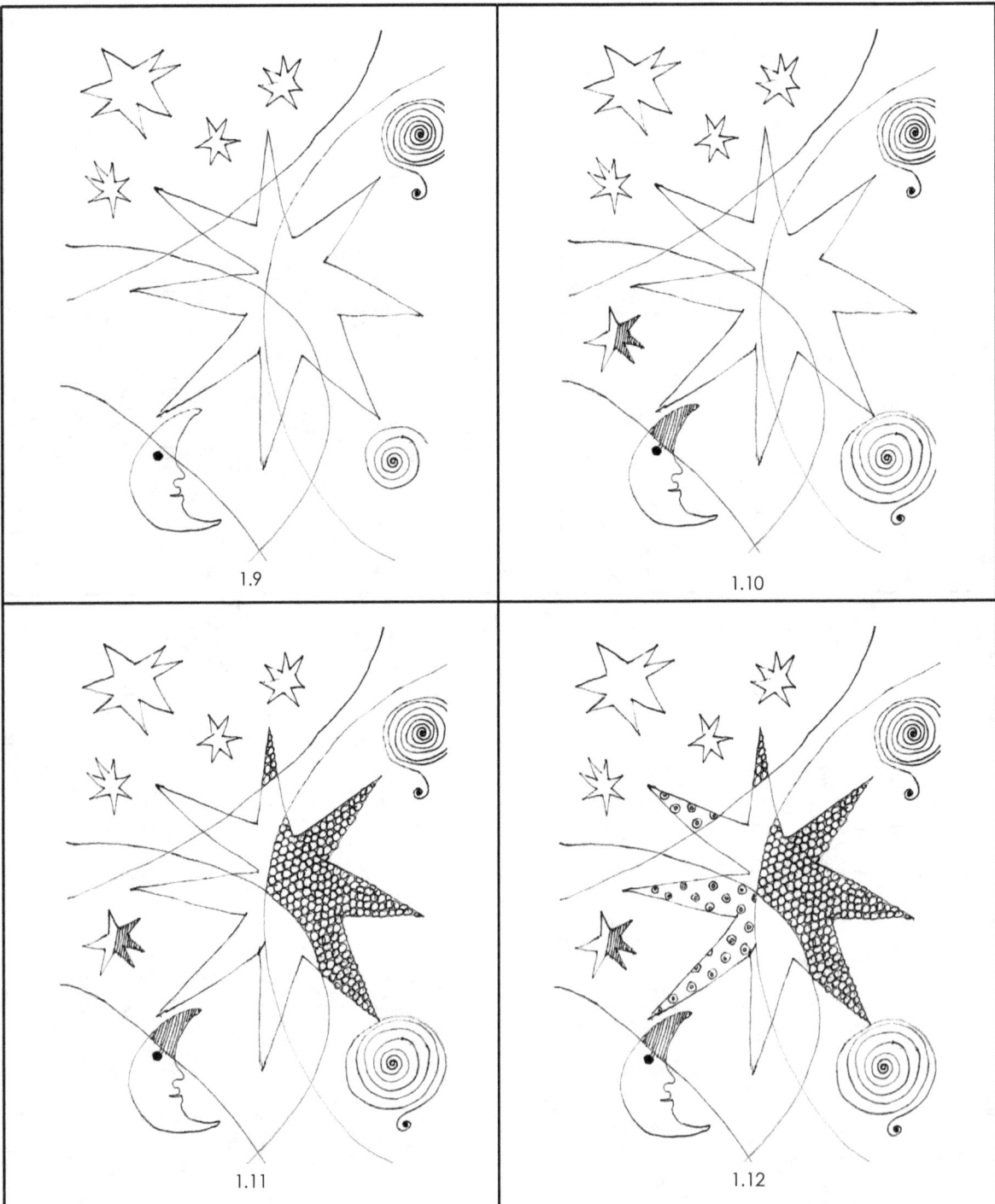

1.9

1.10

1.11

1.12

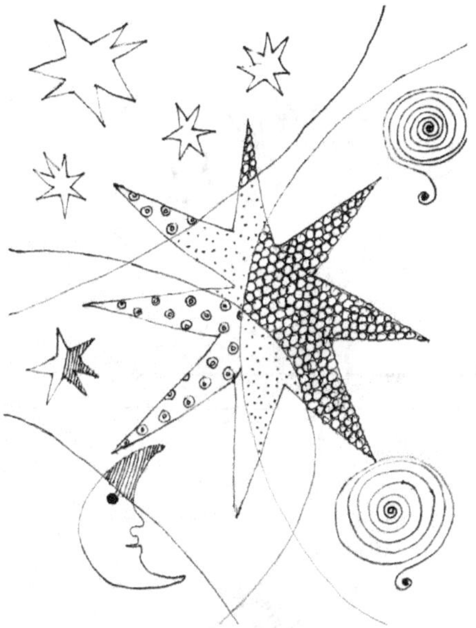

1.13

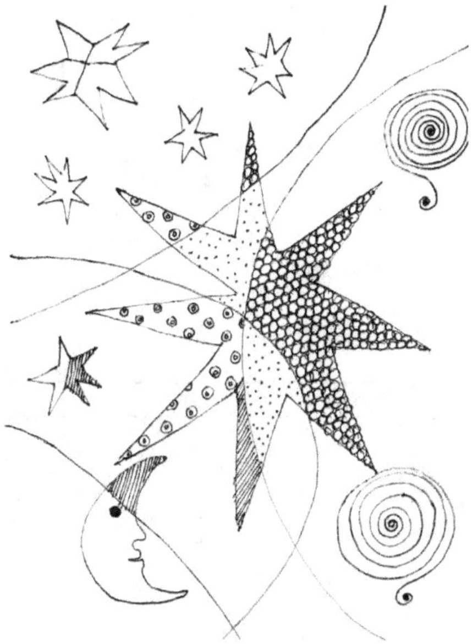

1.14

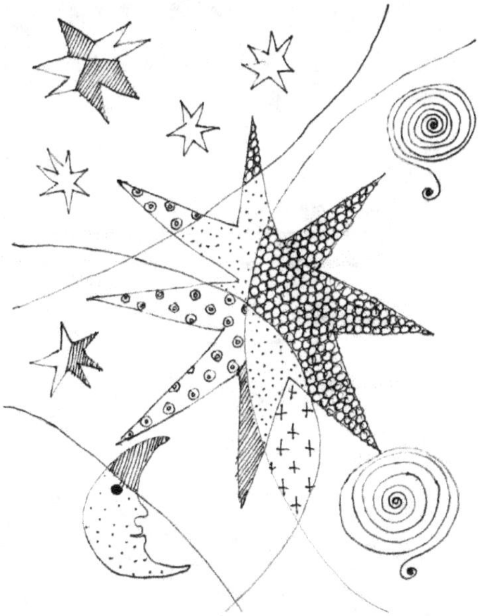

1.15

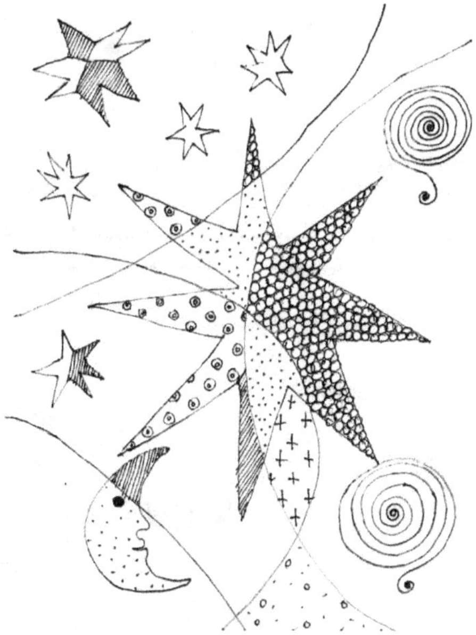

1.16

To learn how to draw patterns, used in this drawing, see pages 17 and 24.

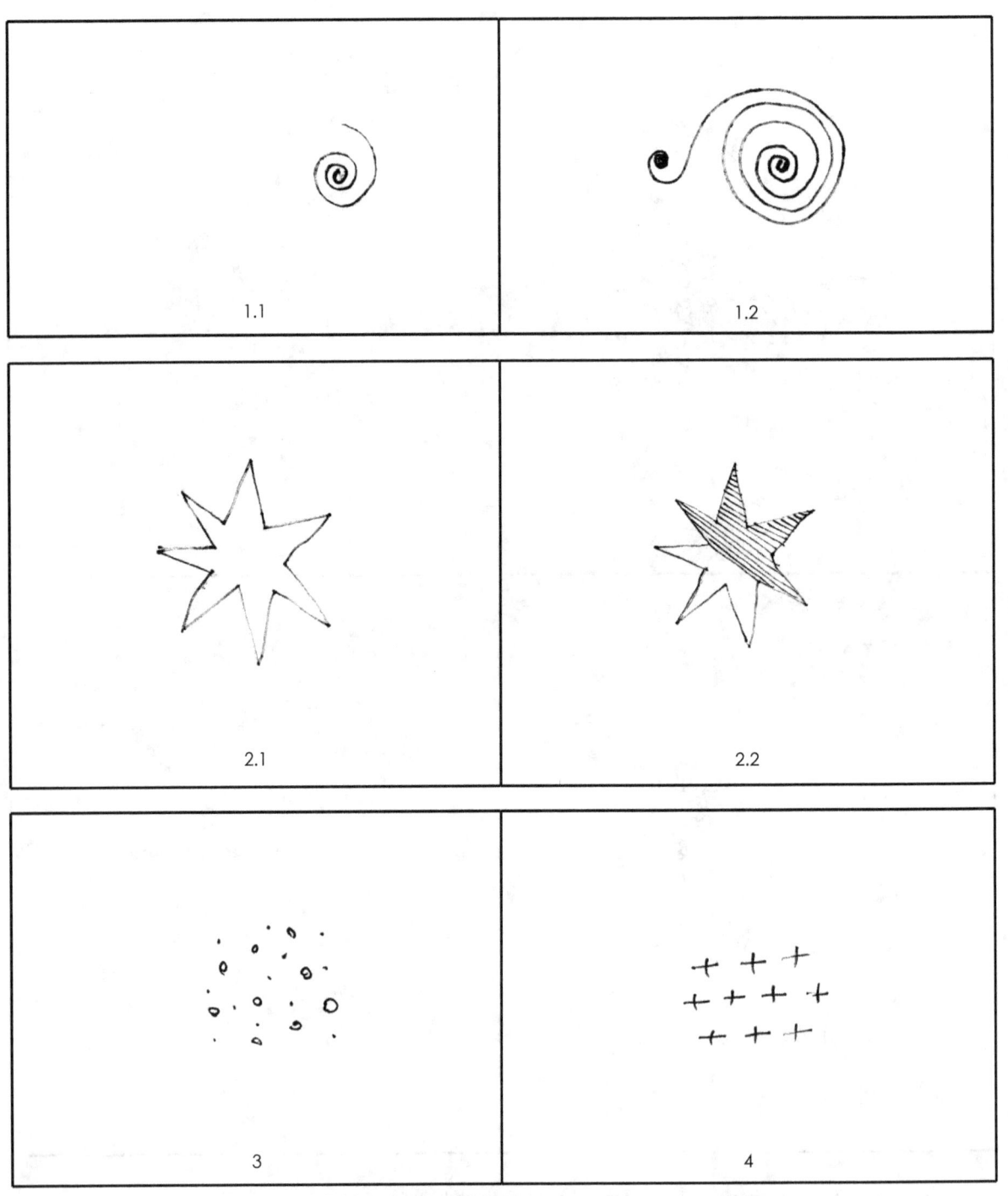

1.1

1.2

2.1

2.2

3

4

How to draw NeoPopRealism abstract "Zig & Zag"

W hat is Zigzag? Traditionally a "zig" points in the left direction - "/" and a "zag" points right "\". Zigzag is a basic decorative pattern. The abstract drawing "Zig & Zag" includes many different patterns, including zigzag.

The following pages will show you how step-by-step with ink pen to draw abstract "Zig & Zag." Each following image includes new details. Remember, that you need no eraser. If you made a mistake, it will disappear with the following repetitive patterns that will make your drawing beautiful and the whole composition balanced. The complete drawing looks like this:

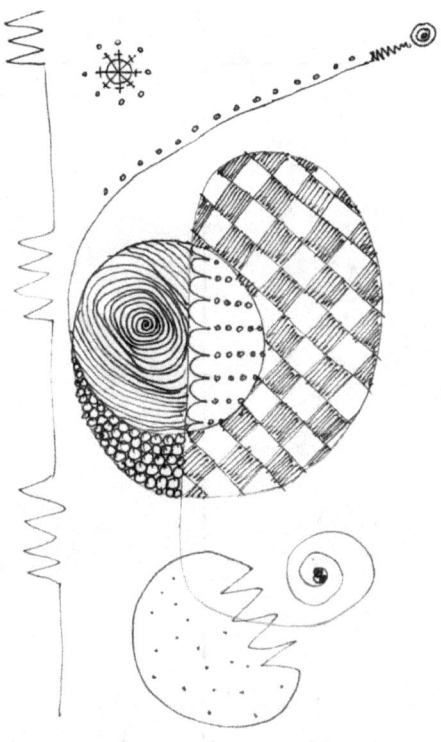

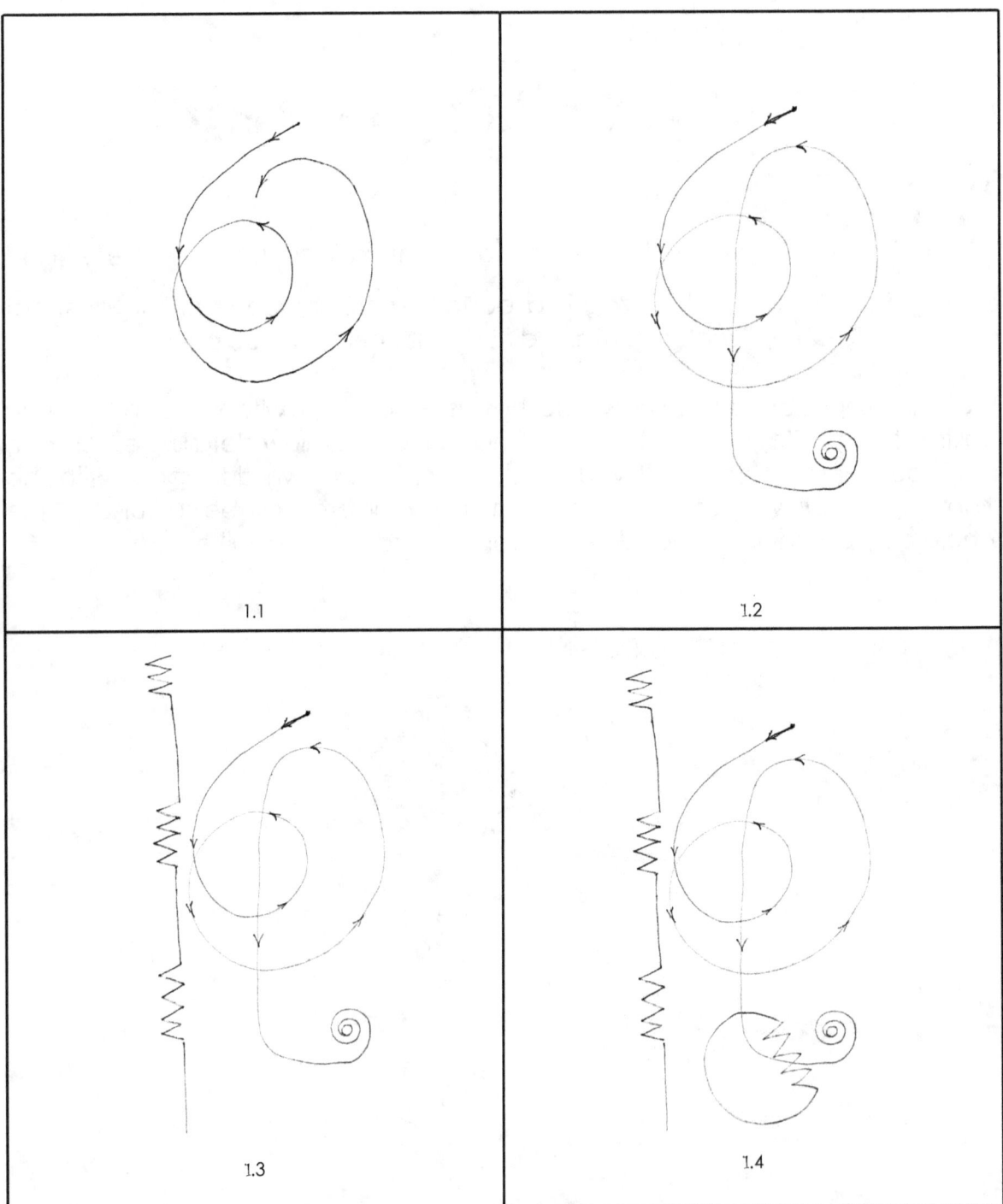

1.1

1.2

1.3

1.4

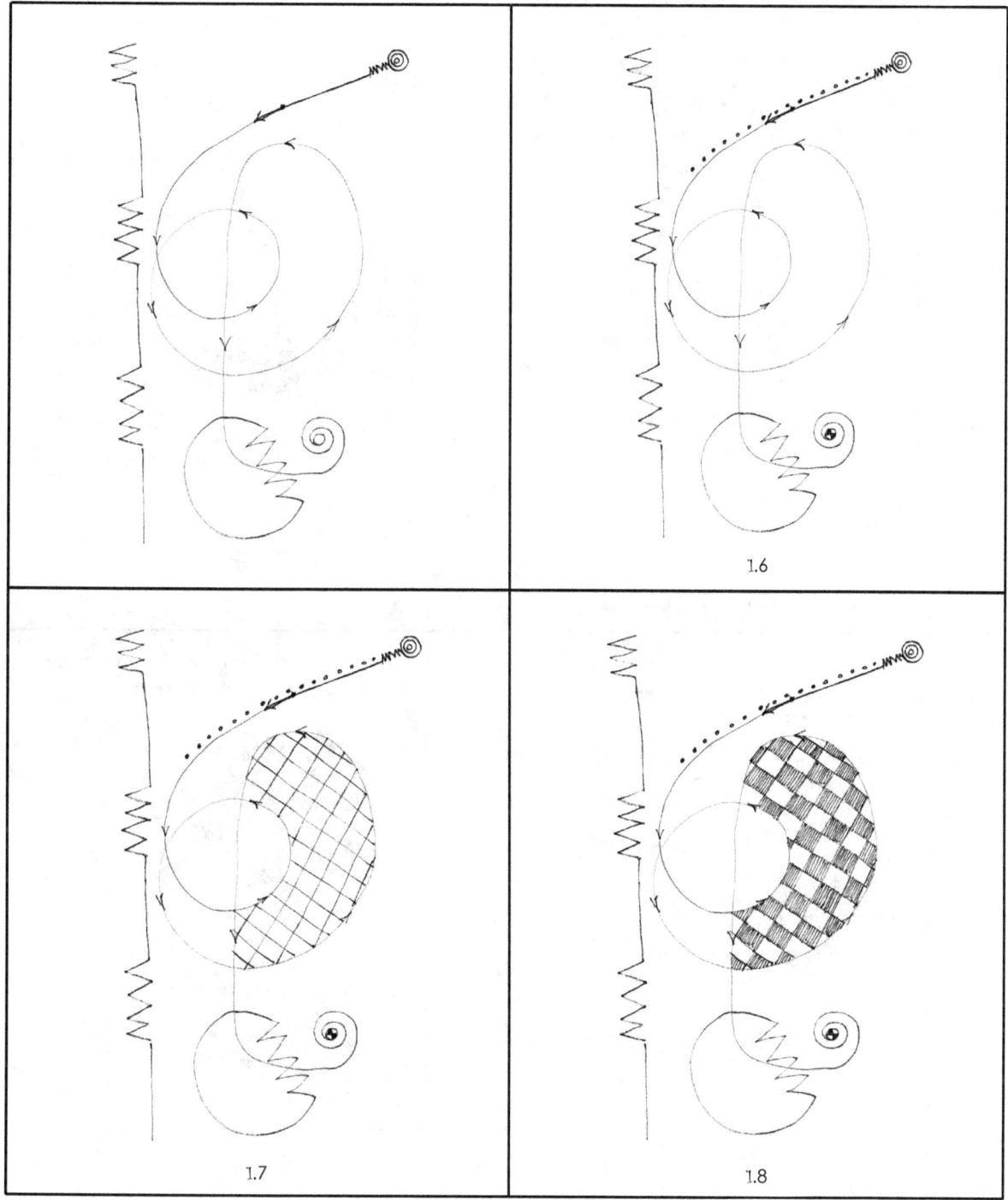

1.6

1.7

1.8

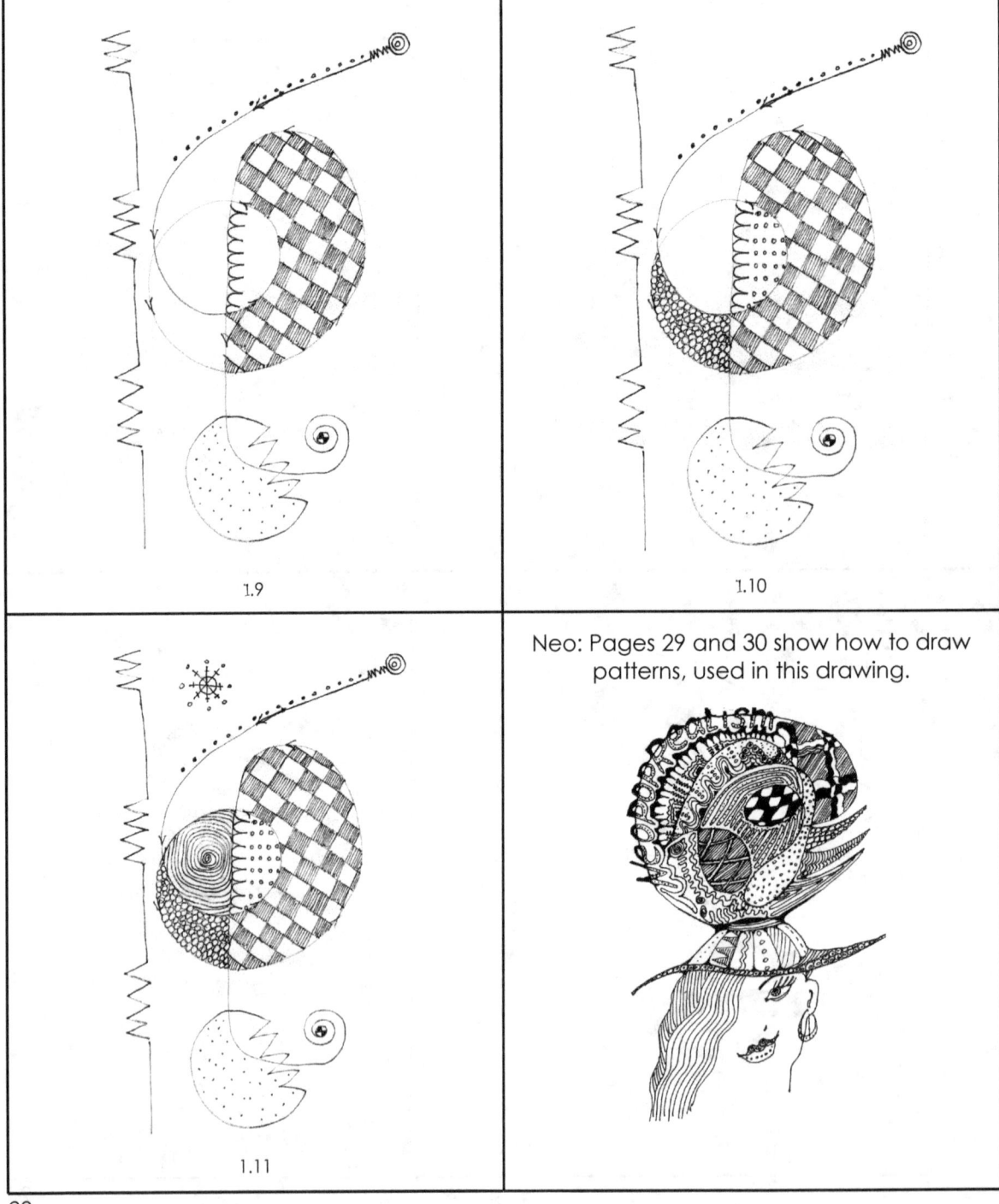

1.9

1.10

1.11

Neo: Pages 29 and 30 show how to draw patterns, used in this drawing.

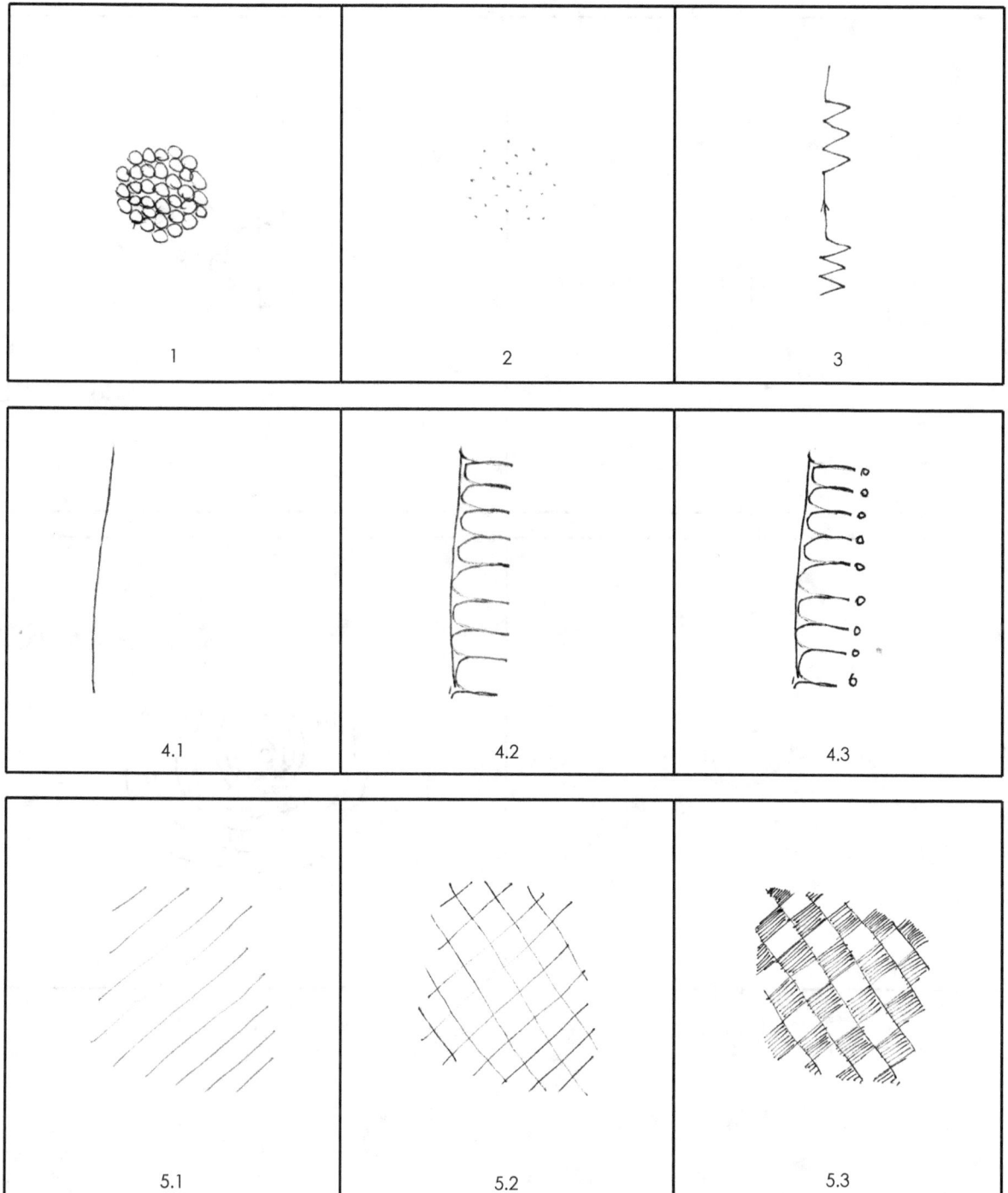

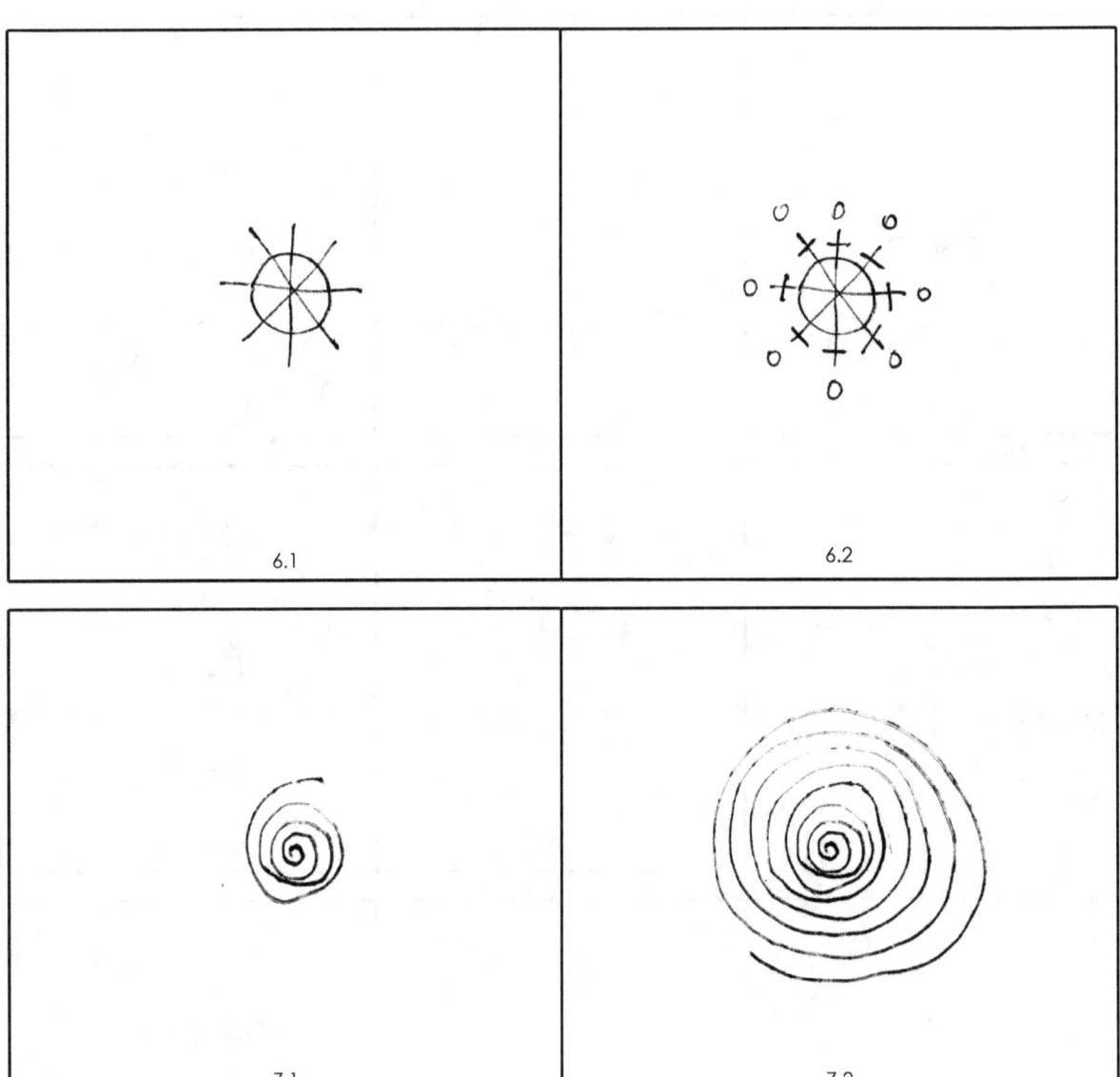

6.1

6.2

7.1

7.2

Your Patterns Gallery

The following pages are for you to create different repetitive patterns, which later you will use in your drawings. Create any patterns you wish, use zigzags, circles, triangles, squares, rectangular, lines, and dots, their combinations and variations. Be creative, develop your artistic skills.

1	2	3
4	5	6

7	8	9
10	11	12
13	14	15
16	17	18

19	20	21
22	23	24
25	26	27
28	29	30

31	32	33
34	35	36
37	38	39
40	41	42

Your exercising pages

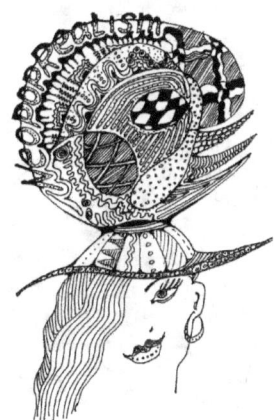

Neo: Pges 39-46 are for you to draw images here and now, from its beginning to end.

Follow all instructions and no doubts, you will make some wonderful drawings.

Preparation:
~ Get your ink pen.
~ Chose size of paper you would like to use.

The Process:
~ Draw the crossing lines, it will create sections.
~ Fill some or all sections that appeared with different repetitive patterns. If you already created your *Repetitive patterns gallery* (pages 31, 32, 33), chose your patterns from there.

Enjoy creative process, it is fun and excitement. Focus on details, it is important. Play with line and repetitive patterns! See samples before you start your drawing (pages 36-37).

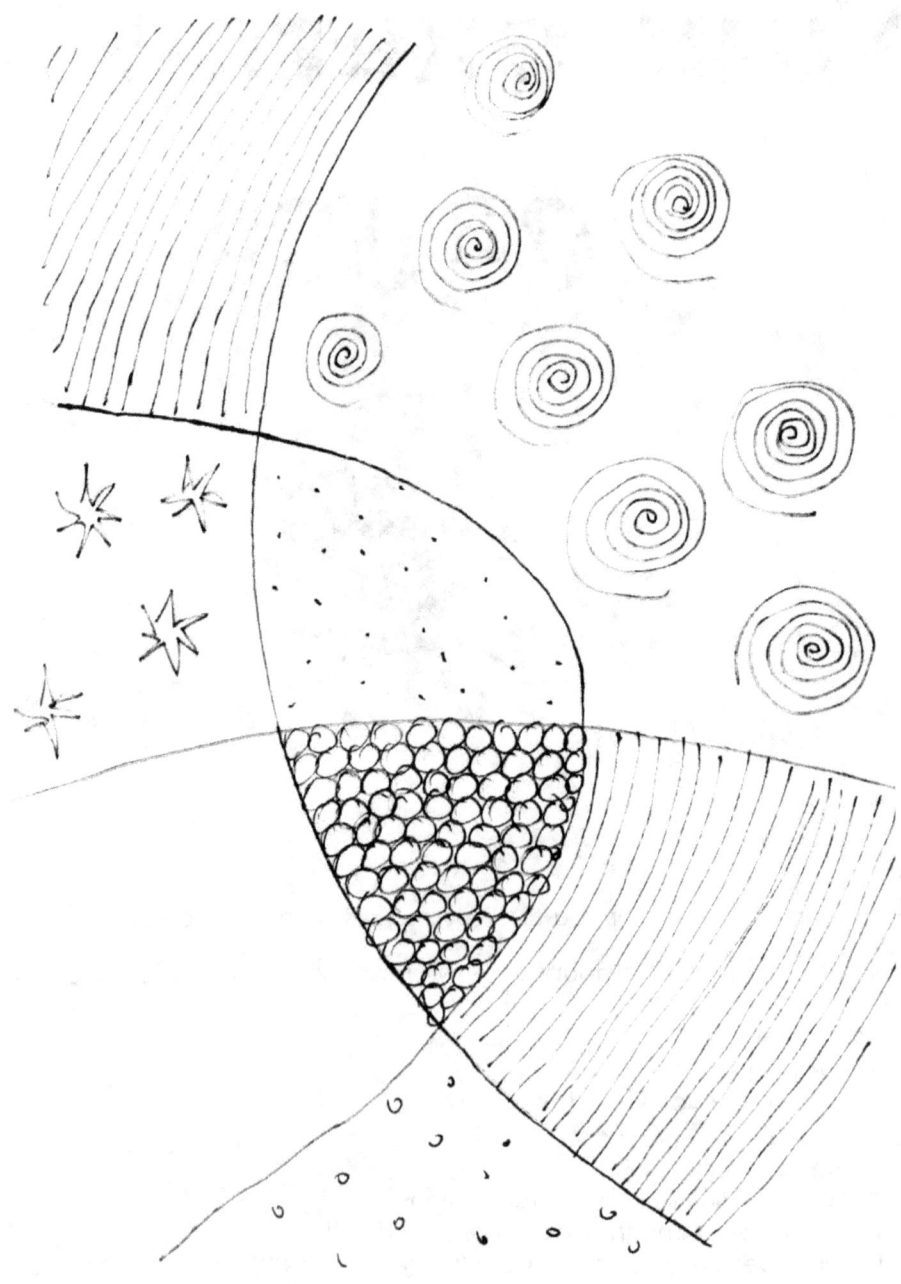

Sample 1

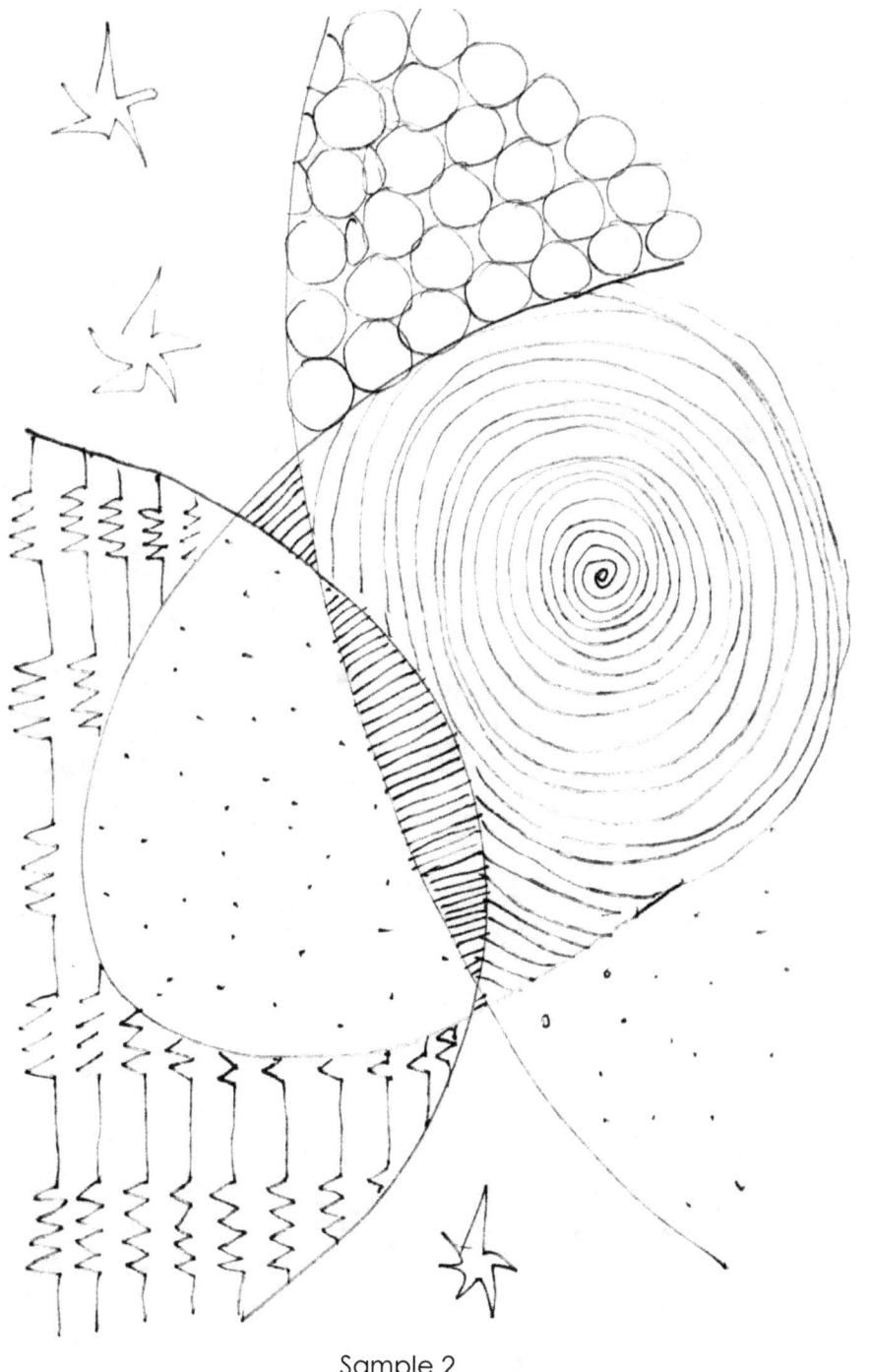

Sample 2

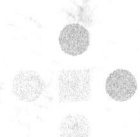

A story you should know

What you have learned in a simple way today, is the ink drawing style, which artist Nadia Russ created long time ago, in 1989. Then, she lived not in the United States yet, but in a capital of Russia, Moscow, located far away, on another continent. And you were then also not in the United States, you were not even on this planet yet, and your parents even didn't meet.

Nadia Russ was very happy about her invention. She exhibited her artworks in famous Manege and wanted to come to the United States, from where she could announce worldwide this new way of the artistic expression she created. She wanted to spread this way of drawing ink images with the line and repetitive patterns without eraser among the all good people.

First time she came to the United State in 1992, but then she didn't speak English. Second time she came in 2000. In 2002, Nadia Russ left her artworks to David Shwaery, President of the Pawtucket Arts Council, and his partner Clifford Cone to exhibit her work in art exhibition in Rhode Island, where they both live. Two weeks later, Clifford Cone said to Nadia that her paintings were demolished by the contractors, who came to repair apartment, where she left her artworks with consignment agreement.

It was unbelievable. Nadia Russ was crying. Many times she and her friends called to Shwaery and Cone asking to return her paintings. When Nadia Russ said to David Shwaery that she will tell to police they don't return her art, he said he will tell to police that Nadia Russ didn't pay rent when she rented from him and Clifford Cone their apartment in Fort Lauderdale, Florida (this is how they met). David Shwaery was ready to make up any story to keep Nadia's artwork, including those about not paying rent... As long as Nadia lived in their apartment, she paid monthly $950, sending to 10 Euclid Avenue in Rhode Island checks, issued by JP Morgan Chase Bank.

A few months later, David Shwaery and Clifford Cone returned Nadia Russ her artworks. First, they returned her paintings on canvas and later, in one year, she got back her ink drawings. Under people's pressure (Nadia's friends constantly called to Shwaery telling him that he must return her work) they were unable to steal her work.

Nadia Russ was happy, talented, and friendly, and had many friends. In 2003, she created a word NeoPopRealism and internationally announced the new style of visual arts she invented. Seemed, her dreams came true.

But not everything was easy. In 2002-2004, she was receiving daily 7-8 anonymous emails, infected with spyware. Someone wanted to know her business. . . She recognized these emails, often they contained a word "fail." Perhaps, someone wanted her to fail in something. But she couldn't figure out who was this person until she got one email that contained her age digits. Only David Shwaery at that time knew her exact age. Now, she knew that these spyware-infected emails were coming from Rhode Island, from the President of Arts Council. But Nadia Russ wanted to be sure and she sent to Shwaery email: "I have no secrets, this is my password ... ." She really had no secrets and she gave to him a password to her Yahoo! email account. Next day, all spyware-infected emails stopped, she didn't receive them any more. Then, she thought everybody are her friends and didn't believe in the bad intentions. She shared with Shwaery all her plans on NeoPopRealism art style and happenings. He was President of the Arts Council, and she thought he could help her spread NeoPopRealism nationally, so children and adults could learn it. He didn't help her.
For many years, Nadia Russ was aggressively anonymously attacked online, she lived like in a war zone. She knew where it comes from, but couldn't understand why, until 2011.

In June 2011, by accident, Nadia Russ saw a little craftsmen's book that was teaching how to draw her style's simplified ink images without eraser, using line and repetitive patterns, and meditate. Authors of this book called this style not NeoPopRealism, but "zentangle." Also, in this book was written that this art form was created by not Nadia Russ, but by Rick Roberts and Maria Thomas, who lived in Massachusetts. It was shocking.

Nadia Russ made some research and found out that these two people, who are not artists, created a word "zentangle" right after Nadia Russ announced the style

NeoPopRealism worldwide. First presentation of "zentangle" was… in Rhode Island. Nadia was browsing online and saw recent article about "zentangle" in newspaper *The Westerly Sun*." It said: "…Teachers attending the program [learning how to draw "zentangle"] were able to get Rhode Island Department of Elementary and Secondary Education, credits for a fee."

Nadia Russ understood what happened and why she was attacked all these years. People used her idea, renamed her art style, simplified it (they are not artists), and were teaching its drawing concept grannies and even children through the Elementary and Secondary Education Departments that paid for this education in Rhode Island. They were selling kits, a lot of kits. At the same time, they didn't want Nadia Russ and NeoPopRealism succeeded, because they were their main competitors.

Now, they mired in social awkwardness. Nadia Russ still does not understand why people do bad things; probably, because they are bad people. Good people would never do bad things.

Conclusion for the young siblings: respect old people, but be careful. Not all older people have always good intentions. Some of them fit to this expression: "There's no devil, there's an old man."

NeoPopRealismPRESS

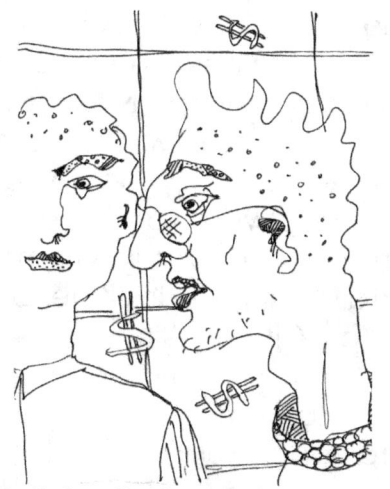

Nadia Russ, *The Crooked*, ink on paper

About NeoPopRealism creator Nadia Russ

Nadia Russ (aka Nadejda Maloletneva) was born into a former professional military officer's family. As a child, she began studying art from famous masters of the past through art books and reproductions, which her mother Vera was collecting in their home. Nadia daily heard about and saw the reproductions of works of Leonardo da Vinci, Michelangelo, Rafael, contemporary Russian artists such as Petrov-Vodkin.

She began painting and drawing seriously in 1989. A few months later, her first ink drawings were exhibited in a group exhibition in famous Moscow's Manege and later, in other Moscow's art galleries. In 1992, she successfully showed her work in New York City.

In 1996-2000, Nadia resided in the Bahamas, where her work gained some special brightness. There, she got her pseudonym to her original 'Nadejda Maloletneva', which was easier to pronounce - 'Nadia Russ'.

In 2000-2001, in Xanadu hotel, she operated her Art Gallery Club 13. In 2000, she moved to the United States, where she lives up until present. January 4, 2003, Nadia Russ created a word NeoPopRealism and manifested internationally new style of visual arts which combines the brightness and simplicity of Pop Art with deep and psychological realism and has graphic nature. Her artworks are in private and permanent public collections including MOYA - Museum of Young Art in Vienna (Austria), Simferopol and Sumy Art Museums in Ukraine, Kinsey Institute of Indiana University (USA), Ukrainian Museum in New York City (USA), WEAM - World Erotic Art Museum in Miami (USA), Schacknow Museum of Fine Arts (USA), Historical Museum of Fort Lauderdale (USA), Lebedyn and Konotop Art Museums (Ukraine), D. Burliuk Foundation (Ukraine), and other.

In 2008-2010, Nadia Russ founded and juried Int'l NeoPopRealism Starz Art competitions. She authored a few art-related books such as "NeoPopRealism Starz: 21st Century ART" two volumes, "New Millennium ART", "Fort Lauderdale 100: A Must-Have Collector's Edition." She is the founder (2007) of the *NeoPopRealism Journal & Wonderpedia*, publications online, dedicated to arts, culture, books, news, celebrities and more. In 2011, she established NeoPopRealism Press, an imprint that publishes the art related books. Nadia Russ lives in New York City and Florida.

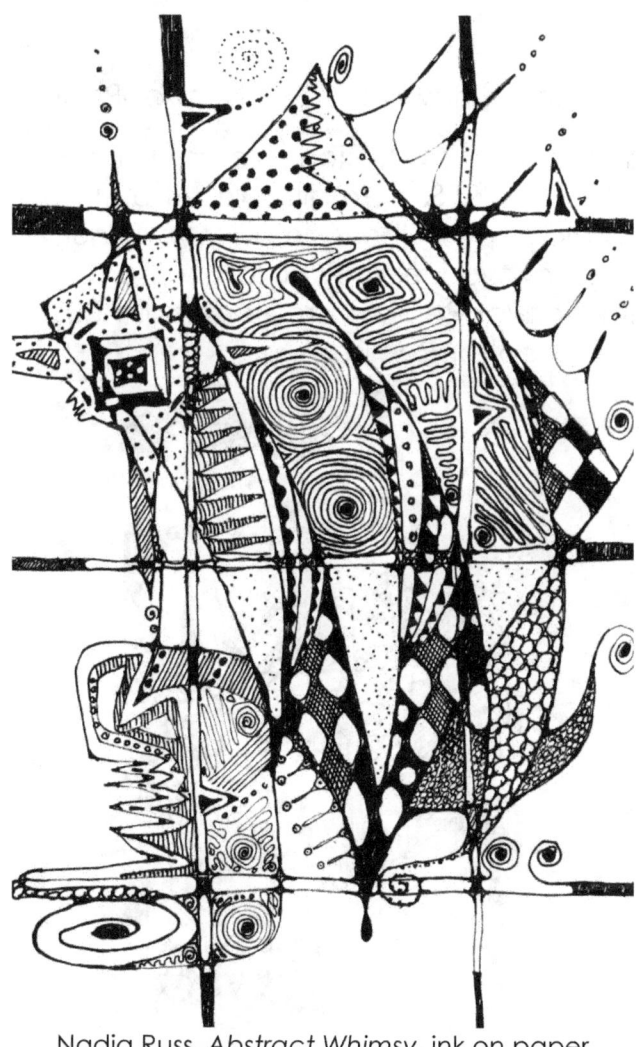

Nadia Russ, *Abstract Whimsy*, ink on paper

CONCLUSION

"WHAT IS ART?"

Now, when you know how to draw NeoPopRealism ink images, you might have your answer to this question. We are happy to hear from you, e-mail us at NeoPopRealismPRESS@Gmail.com. Also, if you or someone from your family has a blog, post there images of your NeoPopRealism ink drawings and a story how you learned to draw them. And, please, mention there this book with NeoPopRealism creator Nadia Russ. Have a wonderful journey to the world of NeoPopRealism!

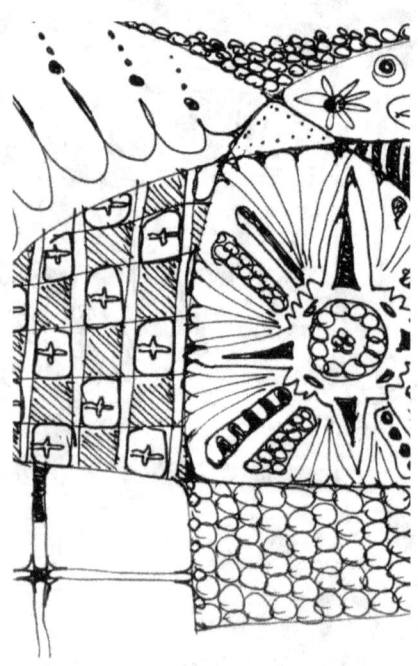

Nadia Russ, *Abstract Meditation (Fragment)*, ink on paper

NeoPopRealism 10 canons for better and happy living

1. Be beautiful.
2. Be creative and productive; never stop studying and learning.
3. Be peace-loving, positive-minded.
4. Do not accept communist philosophy.
5. Be free-minded, do the best you can to move the world to peace and harmony.
6. Be family oriented, self-disciplined.
7. Be free spirited. Follow your dreams, if they are not destructive, but constructive.
8. Believe in god. God is one.
9. Be supportive to those who need you, be generous.
10. Create your life as a great adventurous story.

Created by Nadia Russ in 2004.

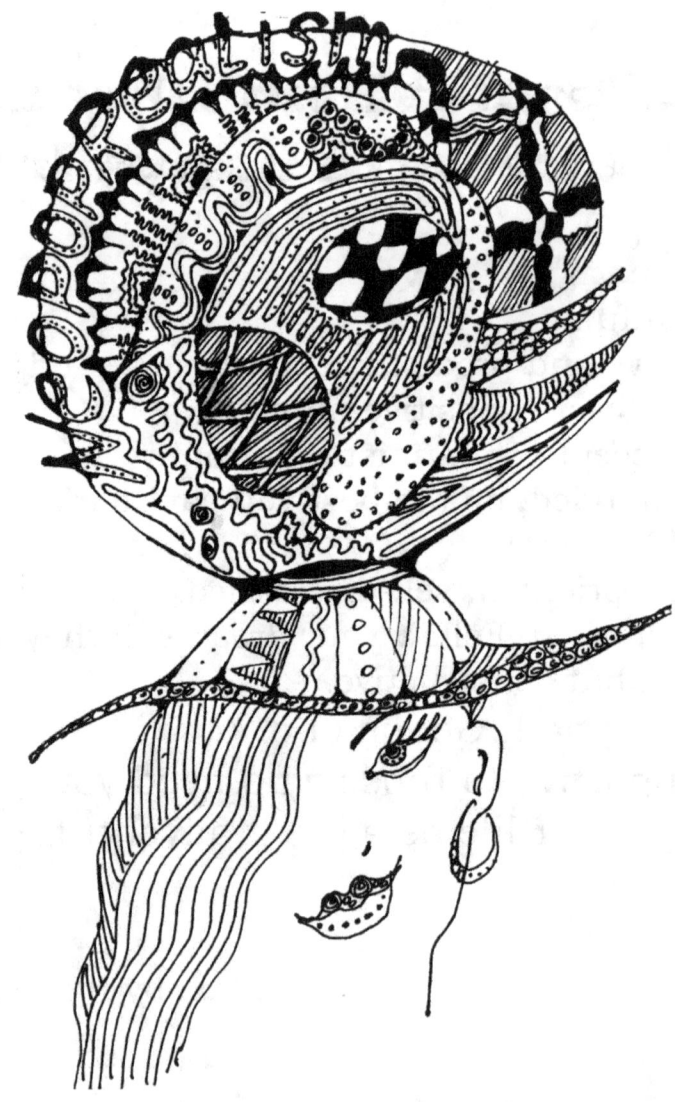

Neo: A Drawing NeoPopRealism ink image is fun. Learn how to draw without eraser. This art style will help you develop intuition and artistic senses. The NeoPopRealism drawing is like game. Get your ink pen, and let's play daily!

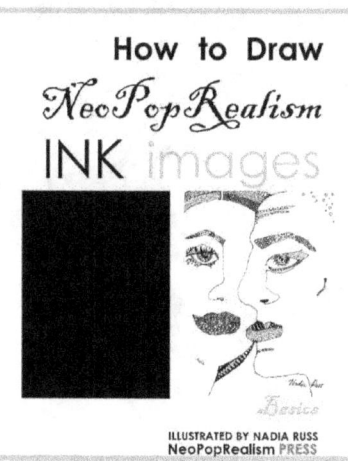

ISBN: 9780615515755
FOR TEENS & ADULTS

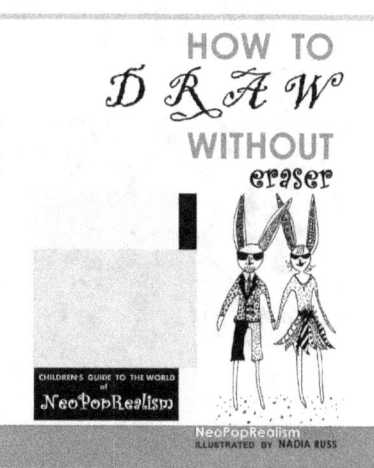

ISBN: 9780615521824
FOR CHILDREN

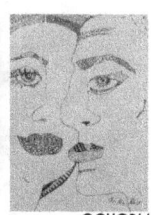

Book "*How to Draw NeoPopRealism Ink Images: Basics*" in Russian translation.
ISBN: 9780615516967

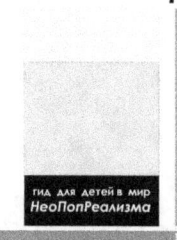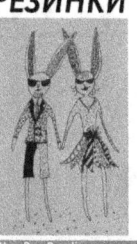

Book "*How to Draw Without Eraser: Backgrounds*" in Russian translation.
ISBN: 9780615523484

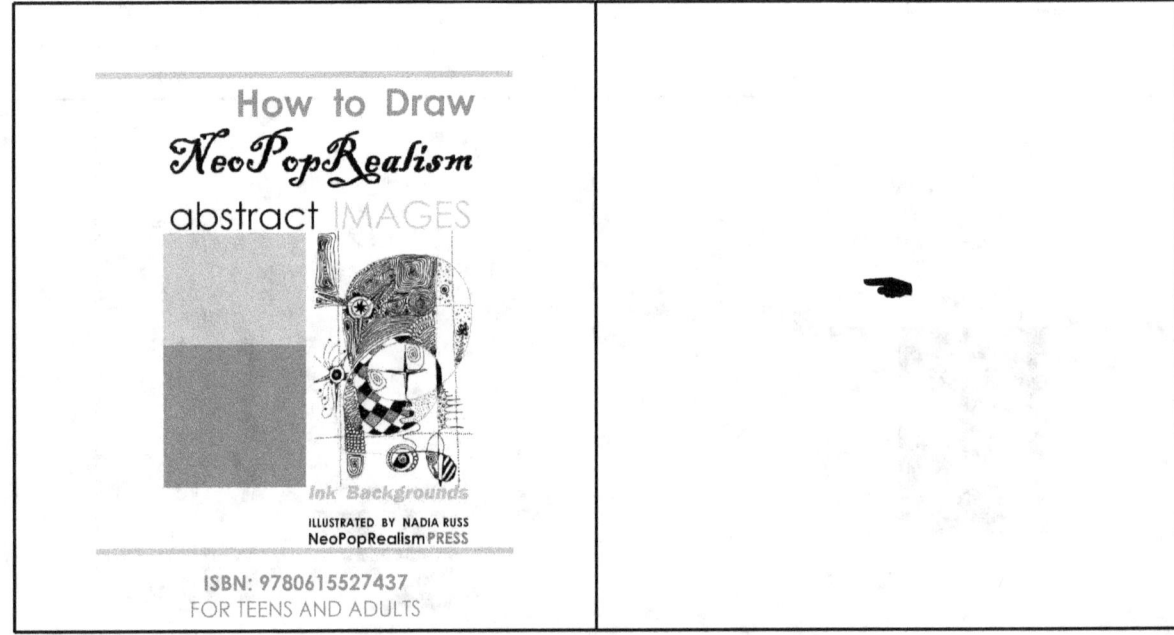

BONUS
PAGES

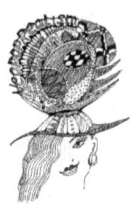

Neo: The following pages are your BONUS! Now you know how to draw the simple NeoPopRealism abstract images and might want to start create the more complicated artwork. These additional pages are for your exercising and improving your artistic skills. Fill each section (or some) of each particular drawing (pages 61-73) with the offered and newly created by you repetitive patterns and their variations. Focus on every detail, learn to create new repetitive patterns and their combinations and variations. Combine circles, squares, triangles and zigzags of different sizes, use your imagination, develop your artistic skills. The next pages 75-79 are for you to create your own abstract images, based on your skills. This type of abstracts Nadia Russ regularly uses as the background for her ink and often acrylic art works.

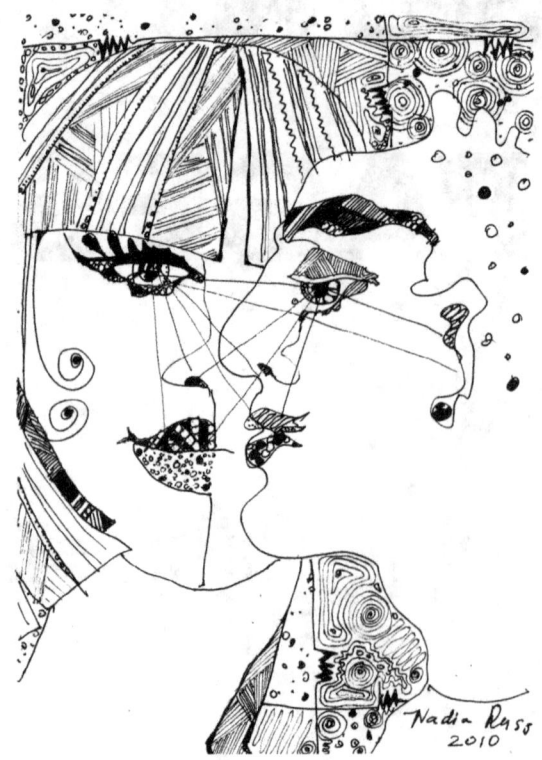

Nadia Russ, *Two Faces*, 8.5"x5.5", ink on paper

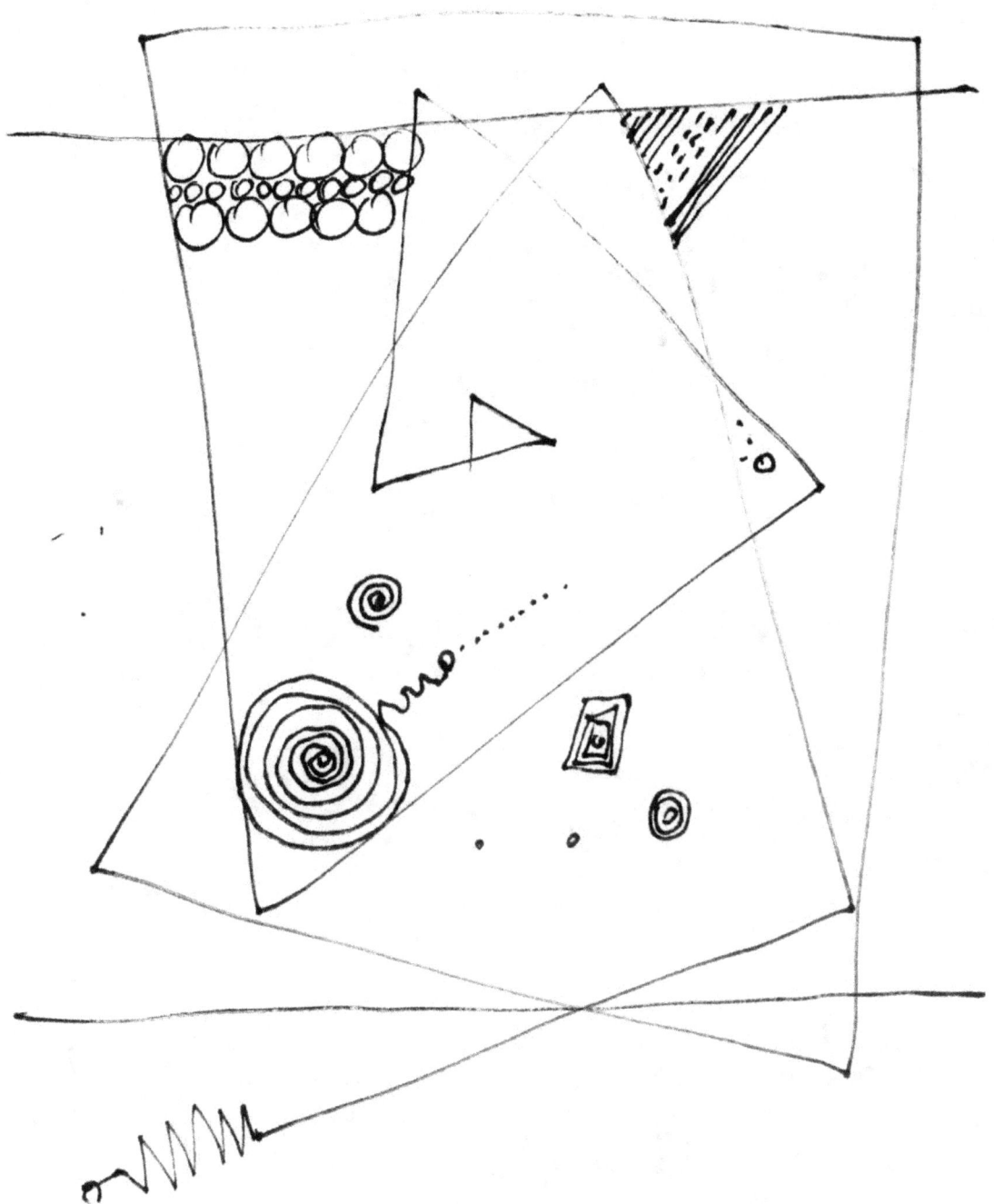

Abstract 1

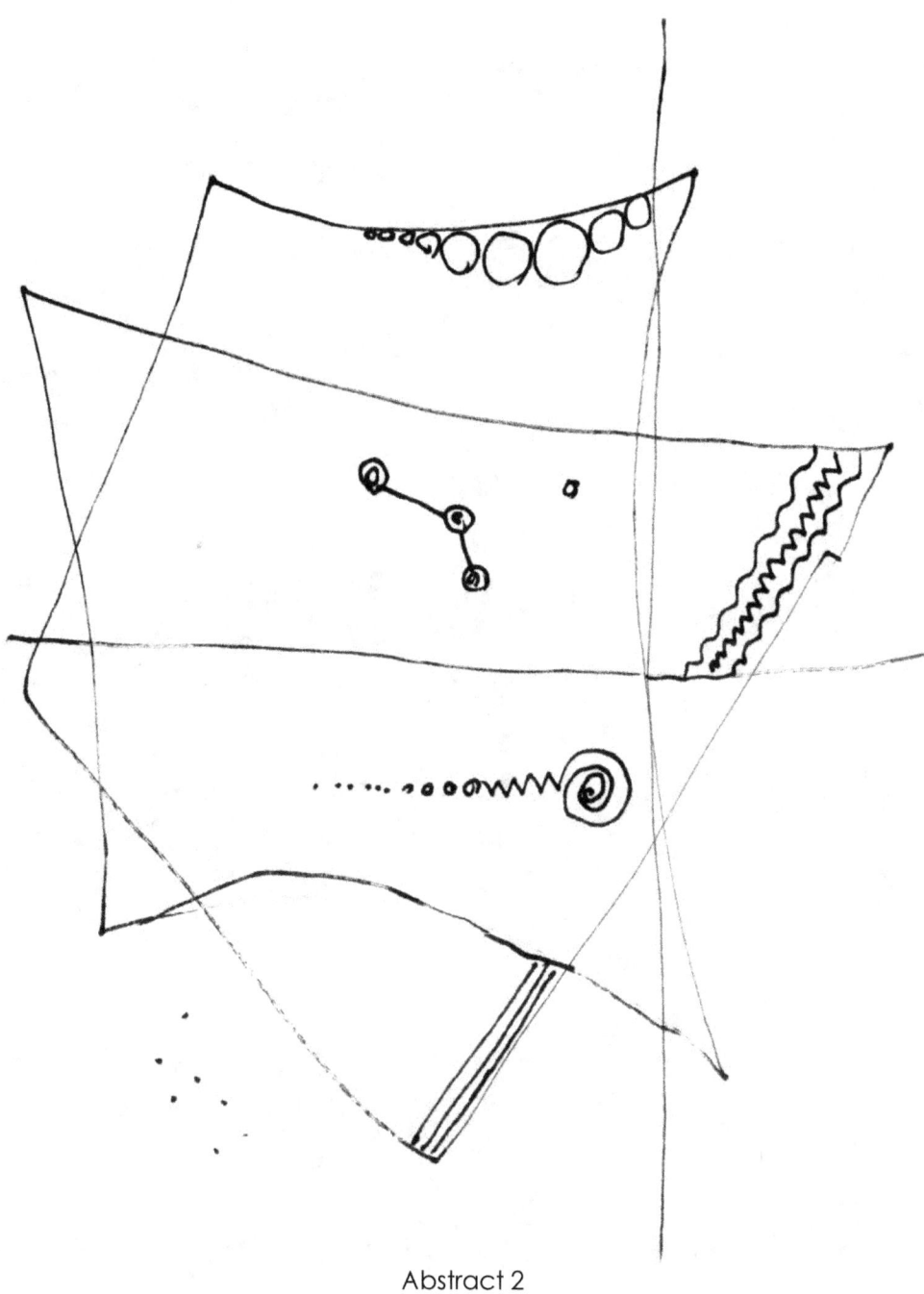

Abstract 2

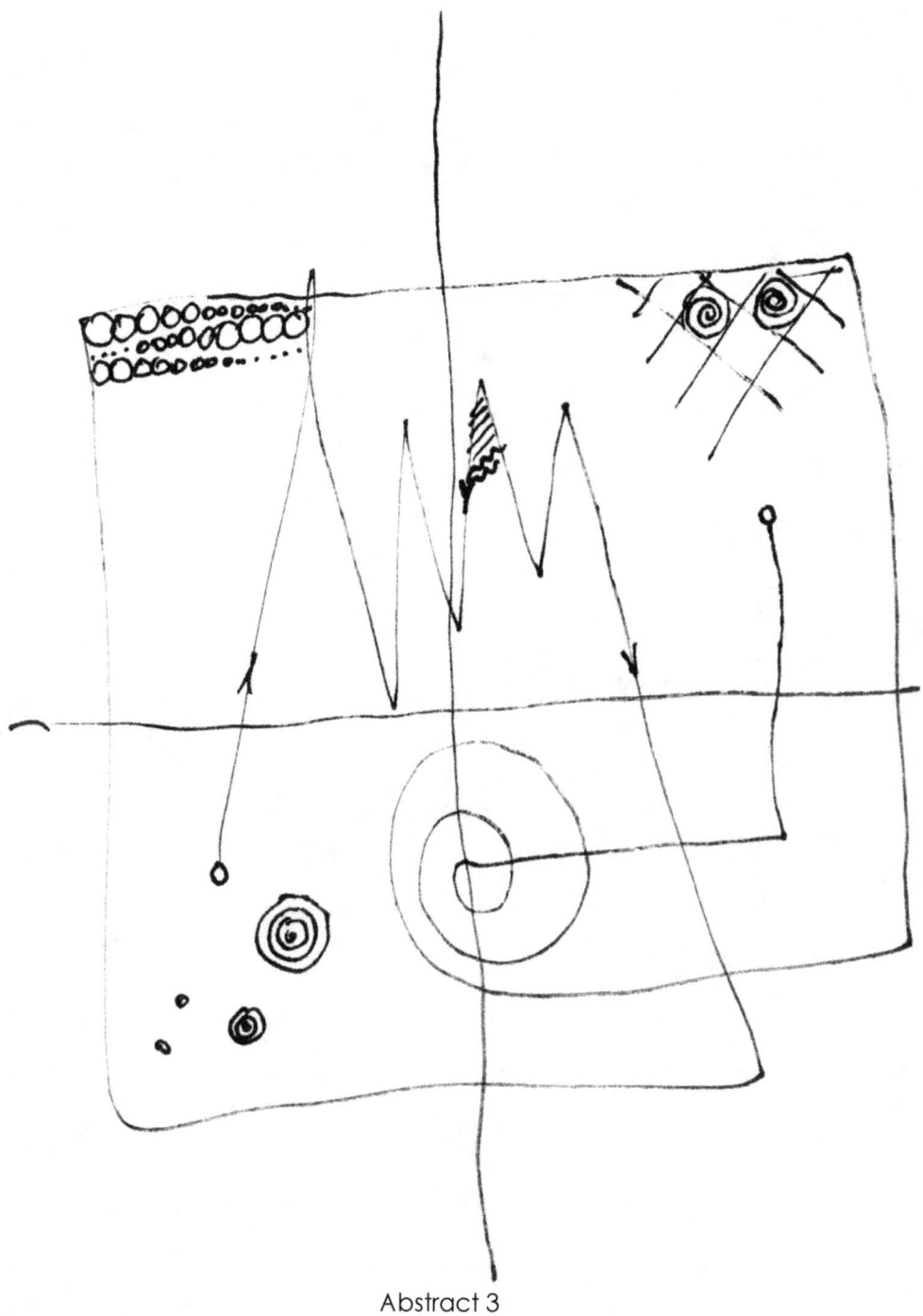

Abstract 3

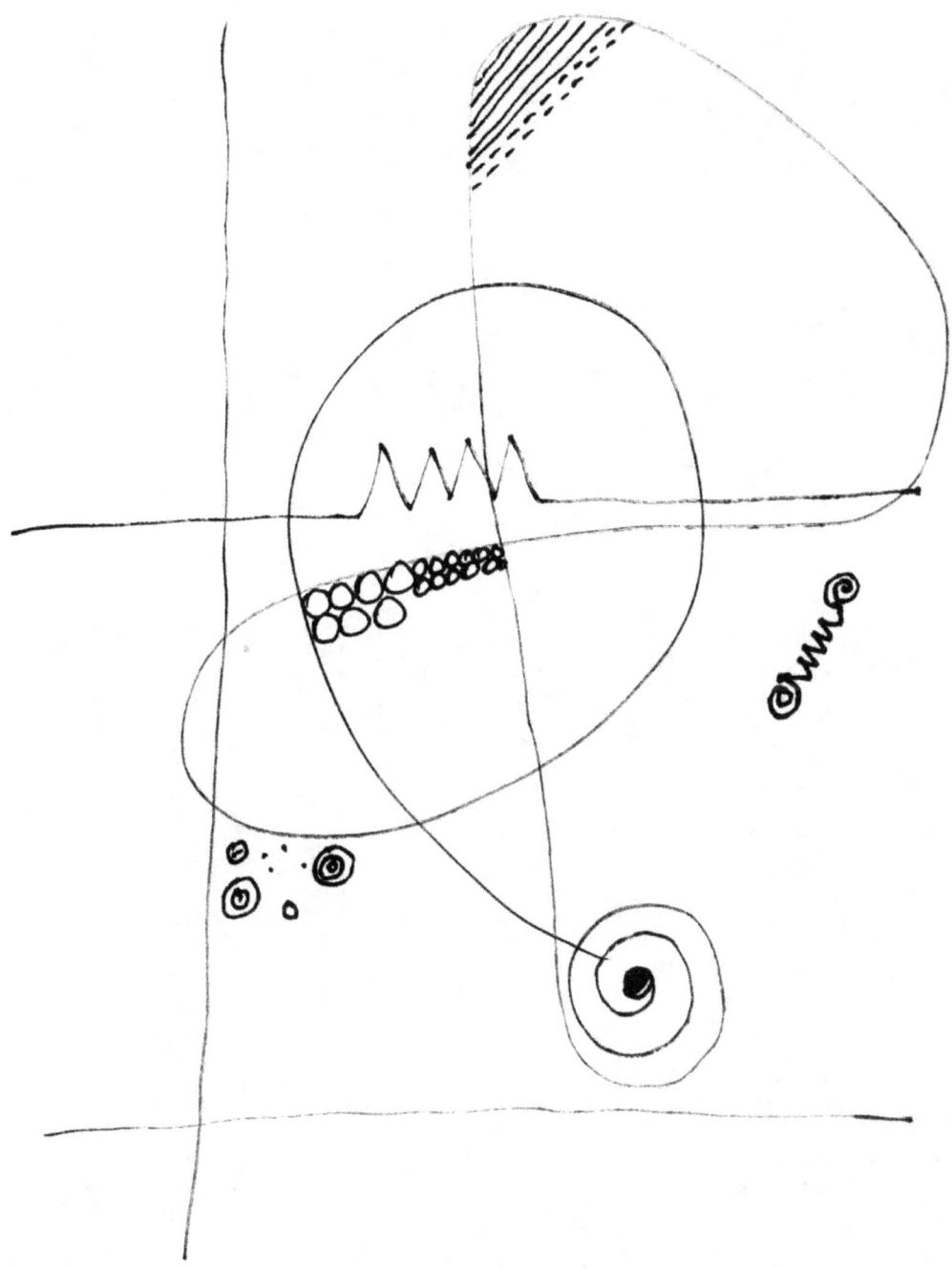

Abstract 4

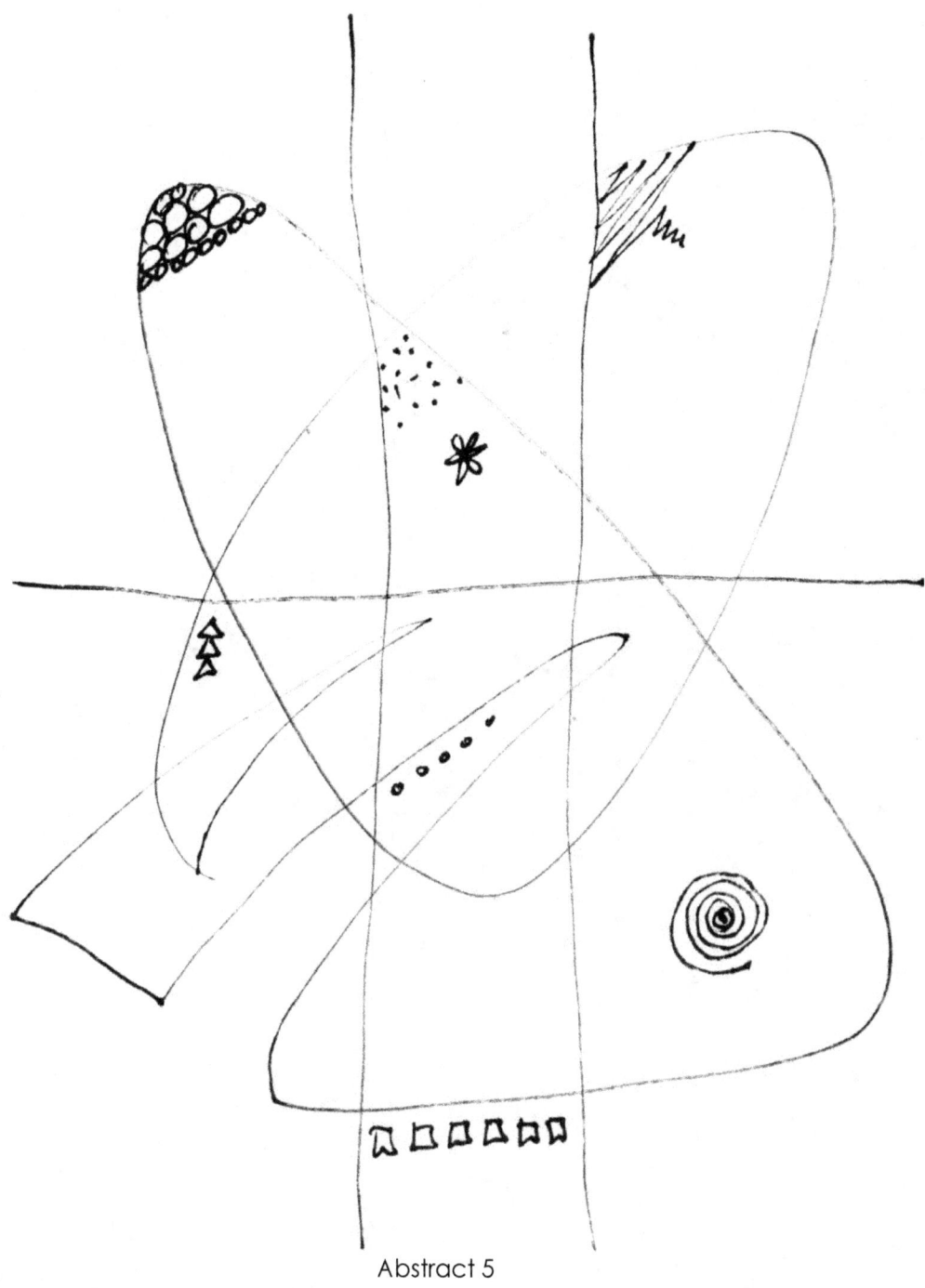

Abstract 5

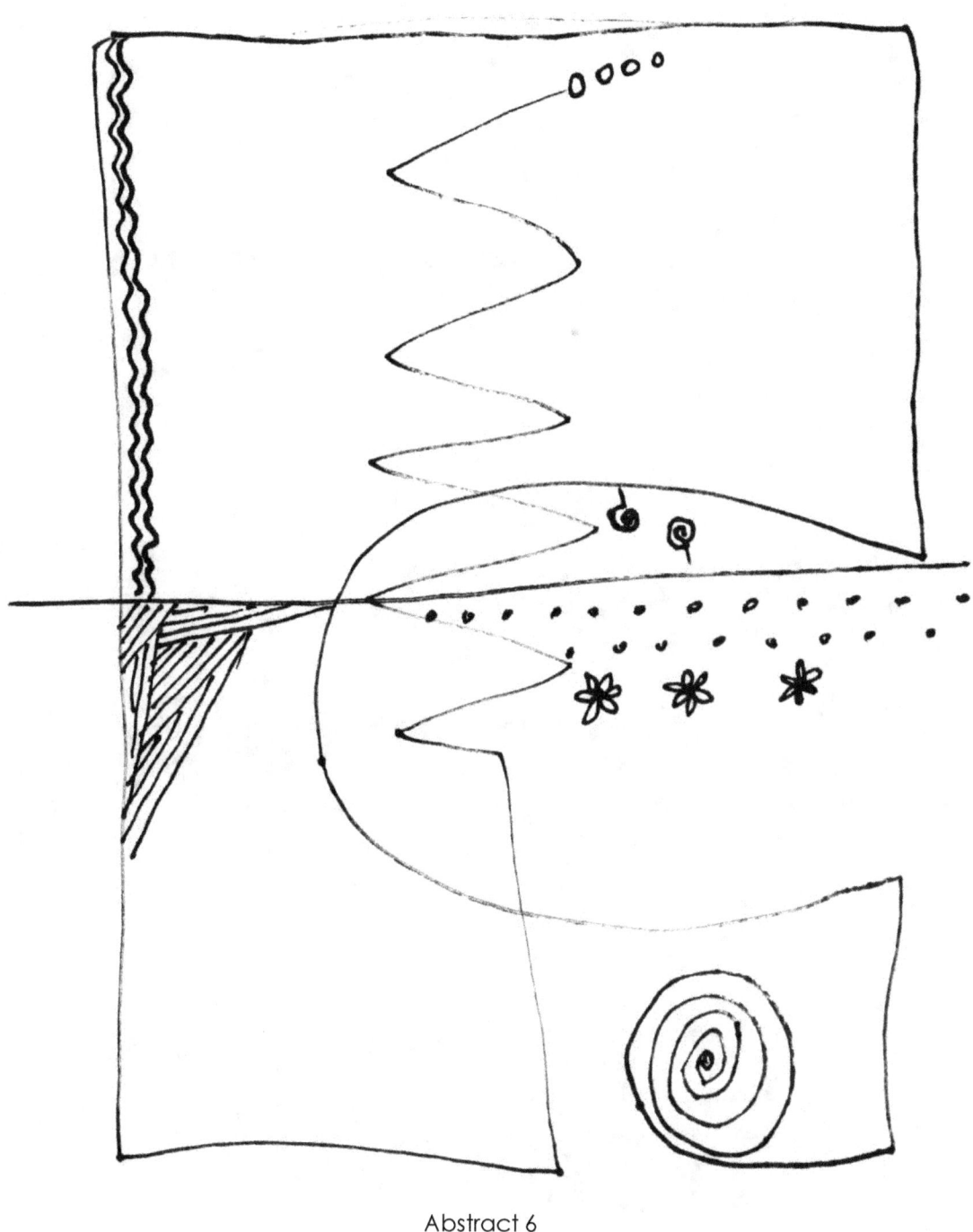

Abstract 6

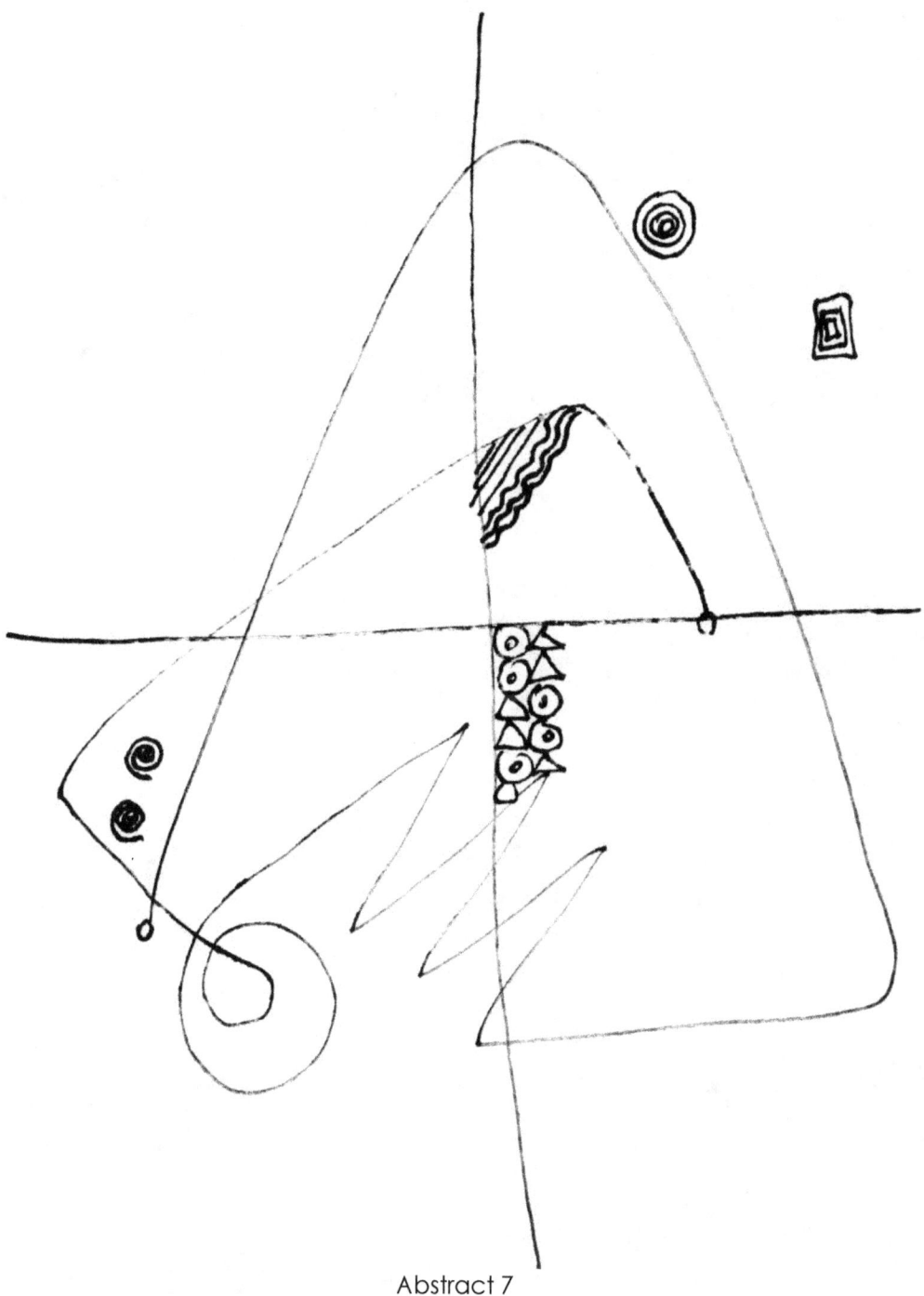

Abstract 7

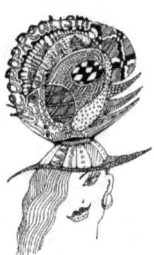

Neo: The following pages are for you to draw more abstract images.